Henry Morton Stanley

Africa, its Partition and it Future

Henry Morton Stanley

Africa, its Partition and it Future

ISBN/EAN: 9783744757942

Printed in Europe, USA, Canada, Australia, Japan

Cover: Foto ©Suzi / pixelio.de

More available books at **www.hansebooks.com**

AFRICA

Its Partition and its Future

BY

HENRY M. STANLEY

AND OTHERS

With an Introduction

By HARRY THURSTON PECK, Ph.D.

Professor in Columbia University

With Colored Map in Pocket

NEW YORK

DODD, MEAD AND COMPANY

1898

University Press
JOHN WILSON AND SON, CAMBRIDGE, U. S. A.

NOTE

The papers collected in this volume were recently prepared by their authors at the request of *The Independent,* in whose pages they first appeared, together with the map which accompanies them. They are reprinted in the belief that they have a unique value at the present time in giving a lucid and authentic statement of facts which are of the very greatest contemporaneous interest, but which have hitherto been practically inaccessible to the general reader.

Contents.

Introduction.

EX Africa semper aliquid novi. So wrote the epigrammatic Roman nearly twenty centuries ago, and each one of these centuries has brought out into still clearer relief the essential truth of his terse saying. Africa, indeed, has always been the Dark Continent from which in every age have come the mysterious and the unexpected. Superficially, to be sure, it is chiefly as a continent of marvels and mysteries that it has been popularly thought of until within the memory of the present generation. In the earliest recorded times and, for that matter, in our own century, its geographical problems have been those which the mention of its name most readily suggested. Circumnavigated by the Phœnicians before the time of Herodotus, whose record of this fact was for a long while discredited; believed for many an age to curve toward the East until it united with Farther India and made of the Indian Ocean an inland sea; containing in its inaccessible depths the source of one of the mightiest rivers of the earth, whose origin was surrounded by a mist

of legend and romance — the wonder-makers
have from time immemorial been active in the
invention and transmission of marvellous stories
regarding this strange continent. Its interior,
which for many centuries no white man ever
penetrated, was peopled with strange creatures
of the unfettered imagination, — with anthro-
pophagi and dwarfs and giants. Mysterious
cities were believed to exist upon the rivers
that lay beyond the Desert. The limitless tropical forests were fancifully held to teem with
dragons and mythical monsters. All travellers, from Herodotus to Mungo Park, brought
back additions to the existing stock of curious
stories to excite the wonder of their contemporaries.

It is not, however, as a wonderland that
Africa deserves the very great attention which
it receives from the minds of men to-day; nor,
in fact, has this been wholly true even in the
historic past. Something more than a pretext
for myth-making it has always been; for, just
as the hot breath of its Desert blowing over the
Mediterranean sensibly affects the climate of the
neighbouring continent, so, to a great extent,
has Africa exercised upon Europe an enduring
influence of another sort, which has varied in degree from age to age, but which has never ceased

to have a very real existence. From the time when Egypt under its native rulers developed an extraordinary civilisation of its own, — a civilisation that knew the arts and sciences, and that had a literature and a philosophy which in many subtle ways found a reflection and a perpetuation in the recorded thought of Greece, — there has never been an age in which in some way the influence of Africa has not been felt in either the political or the intellectual life of Europe. In the Alexandrian Age, Africa was the home of the highest culture, whose scholars laid the foundation of scientific research and literary criticism. In the Roman era, it contained the wealthiest provinces of the Empire. It produced in literature men of high talent, like Fronto and Apuleius, who left a lasting mark upon the history of Roman letters; while the Latinity of the second century is found to be sensibly modified by the example of the great Africans who moulded it and used it to their needs. In the early days of Christianity, Tertullian, the fiery fanatic, and Augustine, whose noble intellect and saintly life are among the most precious heritages of the Church to-day, are but two of the African Fathers whose names are cherished by all Christendom. In the annals of the Later Empire, men of African birth

play so important a part in the political life of
Rome that a distinguished scholar has said that
the whole history of the Roman State at last
resolves itself into the history of a conflict for
supremacy between the African and the German
claimants of imperial power.

It is, however, in our own century that the
direct political importance of Africa has received through circumstances a very general
recognition, — a recognition that has come to
the statesmen of the Old World with a startling
suddenness. The colonisation of the continent
by Europeans began two centuries ago, when
the English established themselves at the Cape
and on the Western Coast; but as this was
before the days of steam, and before the various Powers of Europe had seriously considered
a systematic colonial policy, the settlement at
the Cape assumed no very real importance, any
more than did the fact that men of Dutch descent had occupied the territory on the Orange
River, or than did the existence of the petty
trading-stations which Portugal established. In
the latter half of the present century, however,
Europe has awakened to a knowledge of some
very obvious facts. The first of these is the
necessity of finding some outlet for its own ex-
cessive population, and, in the second place, the

need of new markets for European trade. A recognition of these facts has greatly enlarged the scope and modified the nature of continental policy. A desire for colonies has come upon the rulers of the greatest nations. Russia long ago found a natural outlet for expansion in those vast Asiatic territories adjacent to her own domain; but France and Germany were forced to look elsewhere. The greatest islands of the South Pacific had already been secured by England; the American Republic haughtily barred out from the Western Hemisphere all European colonists who sought to carry to new homes their old allegiances. There remained, therefore, only Africa still unpossessed, essentially unprotected, and presenting possibilities such as might tempt alike the military and the naval strategist, and attract the notice of the resourceful trader. Great tracts of country, teeming with undeveloped riches, lay unclaimed. There were millions of acres of fertile land watered by noble rivers; there were tropical forests that gave promise of untold wealth in the shape of exotic woods and spices; there were also vast regions still unexplored, but described by rumour as rich in gold and silver and precious stones.

Upon the soil of Africa, therefore, in the past fifty years there have been unfurled the flags of

Introduction.

many nations, until now there is very little of its
territory that remains unoccupied or unclaimed
by European States. France gained her earliest foothold on African soil in Senegal in the
seventeenth century, but she won a more valuable possession in Algeria soon after 1830, when
she began the suppression of Algerine piracy,
and ended with the conquest of the entire
country, following up this acquisition later with
her protectorate over Tunis, her annexation of
Madagascar, and the extension of her sphere
of influence over Central Africa through the
French Sûdan and the French Kongo; so that,
roughly speaking, she now claims supreme
control of the territory extending from Algeria
to the head waters of the Niger, having seized
in 1893 the so-called holy city of Timbuktu,
the great trade-mart for the interior, and ultimately to be united with Algiers or Biserta by
a railway nearly two thousand miles in length.
The German occupation of Africa is much more
recent, since it dates only from 1883, when the
imperial flag was raised on the West Coast, and
almost simultaneously in East Africa, in Togoland, and the Cameroons, leaving a certain un-
defined sphere of influence south of the Portuguese Angola. The next year, 1884, saw the
Italian flag hoisted upon African soil where

Introduction.

Italy has lately lost so much and gained so little in attempting to maintain herself upon the strip of sea-coast called Eritrea, and to acquire a sphere of influence at the expense of Abyssinia. The interesting experiment, called the Kongo Free State, was begun in 1885, when its existence under the sovereignty of the King of the Belgians was recognised by the Congress of Berlin. Portugal, whose claims were once so great as to include an immense tract extending across the entire continent, has been restricted to the possession of two or three small strips of territory that are still not very accurately defined.

The seizure and the gradual occupation of these portions of Africa have, as already stated, been fraught with momentous consequences to the political conditions of Europe, inasmuch as new interests have thus been created whose conflict has been a source of contention and of endless friction among the colonising States. When the so-called territorial "scramble" began, the balance of European power had been very carefully adjusted and was holding the opposing forces in a very delicate equilibrium. The Triple Alliance between Germany, Austria, and Italy had been offset by the less formal, though in many respects no less real,

entente existing between France and Russia;
while England, uncommitted to either combination, and thus left free to cast her enormous
power into either scale, enjoyed remarkable
advantages from the standpoint of diplomacy.
The colonisation of Africa, however, has already
materially changed the conditions that existed
so lately as five years ago. As soon as other
nations began to push their way into the African continent, and to attempt the delimitation
and definition of their new possessions, they
found themselves at many points brought into
a direct and sometimes an almost irreconcilable
conflict with each other. Their hinterlands
and spheres of influence often overlapped; and
the difficulties of the situation were frequently
enhanced by the duplicity of the native chiefs,
who made treaties with one or the other of
the different rivals, pledging to each and all,
with utter irresponsibility, the very same concessions. There were also conflicting claims of
discovery and of actual occupancy to be adjusted ; and as the territories in question were
often so little known as to be incapable of exact
definition, another element of confusion super-
vened. But in this clash of interests it has
been England which in a political sense has
suffered most. Her earlier exploration and

actual possession of territory made her the one
power whose presence oftenest blocked the way
of the later colonisers, so that at the present
time there has been roused against her the bit-
ter jealousy not only of France, her traditional
enemy, but of Germany, her traditional ally as
well; while again and again her bold explorers
have crossed the tracks of the Portuguese, and
have at times been on the verge of actual military conflict. Thus, to-day, the political results
of the scramble for African territory are very
striking. In the first place, Italy, by undertaking in Abyssinia a task beyond her power
to perform, has demonstrated her military weak-
ness and administrative incapacity, so that she
has ceased to be an actively effective member
of the Triple Alliance. In the second place,
England no longer stands aloof and unembar-
rassed in her colonial ambitions, but is confronted by the opposition of two of the greatest
Powers of the continent, whose enmity to each
other has been appreciably softened by the
acrimony which animates them both in the
presence of their great Anglo-Saxon rival.

It is this phase of the colonisation of Africa
which possesses for most of us the greatest interest and importance; for again and again it
has seemed to involve the possibilities of ac-

tual warfare, and it certainly contains within
itself innumerable elements of extreme danger.
It is, in fact, the critical position into which
England has been brought through her colonial
policy in Africa and Asia that has made her
turn during the past few months to the American Republic as a possible ally against a continental combination, and that induced her to
give not only moral but active diplomatic assistance to this country during the progress of
its war with Spain. It would be a curious out-
come of the entrance of Europe into Africa, if
the partition of African territory should indi-
rectly bring about a federation for defensive purposes of the entire English-speaking race.

During the past ten years, the periodicals of
all countries have teemed with description and
argument as to the partition and the future of
Africa. The press has recorded from week to
week the progress of discovery and colonisation, and it has brought to the minds of every
one the acuteness of the rivalry which exists
between the claimants for colonial supremacy.
Amid all the mass of geographical statistics,
and in the maze of controversy that has been
woven about the aims and motives of the different Powers, it has been almost impossible for
even the most intelligent person to gain a defi-

nite understanding of the existing facts. The remoteness of the scene and the paucity of authentic information have been utterly bewildering. All that most of us have known is simply the broad fact already stated, that the greater Powers of Europe are now confronting one another in a contest for empire in a continent that is still but half explored. It was a happy thought, therefore, which led to the preparation of the papers reprinted in this volume. Taken together they constitute a brief, authoritative, and lucid statement of the African situation as it is to-day. They describe with perfect clearness the possessions actually held by each of the rival Powers; they define and explain the claims which have brought these Powers into opposition; and they give an interesting forecast, from the point of view of each nation, of the manner in which the complicated problem is likely to be solved. The writer of each paper is a specialist whose knowledge is a first-hand knowledge, and who has had access to all the sources of official information that exist; and the fact that he shows a certain half-unconscious national bias in his statements, merely gives additional interest to what he has to say. No volume that has yet appeared has thrown such light upon a subject which in all its phases appeals

with exceptional force to the reflective mind;
for whether one regards it from a geographical standpoint, or from the side of contemporaneous political history, or as marking an epoch
in the history of civilisation, the whole theme is
fraught with the most striking possibilities.

To many minds the most fascinating feature
of this African complication is to be found in
the attitude of England standing face to face
with so many powerful rivals, and fronting all of
them with the dauntless serenity of the Anglo-
Saxon, holding in a grip of iron all that she has
won, and awaiting with calm confidence the out-
come of the future.   In the great game of
colonial diplomacy she has never lost a point.
Planting herself firmly in Egypt, where she won
an irresistible advantage in 1882 through the
momentary vacillation of the French; trans-
forming that country from a miserable tax-
burdened nest of thieves and cowards into a
prosperous and self-respecting State, whose
sons she has taught to dare as well as to en-
dure; pushing her outposts farther and farther
south, so that her soldiers may at length clasp
hands with the hardy pioneers of the Cape, who
with equal boldness and persistency are forging
toward the North; outwitting her French and
Russian rivals in Abyssinia, and in the West as

well, — no thoughtful person can for a moment doubt that it is she at last who will be the arbiter of Africa.   She alone, indeed, has the instinctive genius for colonisation, for her sons alone are unfettered by the oppressive and brutal militarism which blights the colonies of Germany, and by the timid inefficiency which makes the Frenchman in a foreign land so helpless and so ill at ease.   No one can refuse to believe that she will repeat in Africa the history that she has made in North America and in Australasia; that in the end it is Anglo-Saxon civilisation which will give to the Dark Continent the light of free institutions, of justice, and of law; and that England will once more reap the rich rewards which in the past she has always won through the inestimable service that she has rendered to the cause that is the cause of all humanity.

HARRY THURSTON PECK.

Columbia University,
August the first, 1898.

AFRICA IN THE TWENTIETH CENTURY.

AFRICA IN THE TWENTIETH CENTURY.

BY HENRY M. STANLEY, M.P.

TO draw the horoscope of Africa, and foretell in what condition she will be in 1998, is a rash and risky undertaking; and it is with considerable misgiving that I have ventured to consent to giving you my opinion upon the subject. If I mass them under the term " probabilities " there will be no harm done, while I hope they will be of interest to some of your readers.

In 1798 the whole body of the African continent north of the limited Cape Colony to the Mediterranean countries was absolutely unknown except a thin coast fringe. Bruce had been to the head of the Blue Nile, and Mungo Park had visited Timbuktu; and their lines of travel with Morocco, Algiers, Tunis, Tripoli, Egypt, Abyssinia, and Senegal comprised our knowledge of inner Africa. Despite numerous maps that had been published between the fifteenth and nineteenth centuries the best geographers knew little more of the continent than the contemporaries of Ptolemy, 150 A. D.

What is known of Africa in 1898 is mainly due to the explorations which commenced with Livingstone's journey to the Zambezi in 1854–57. By August, 1884, the basins of the Nile, Kongo, Niger, Zambezi, and Limpopo, together with all the great lakes, were fairly well known ; and since then exploration has been on such a scale that there is now but little left to discover.

In December, 1884, commenced the Berlin Conference, and soon after came the scramble for the bulky continent. We find Africa partitioned to-day as follows: France has secured 3,000,000 square miles, Germany 884,000 square miles, Great Britain 2,190,000 square miles, Italy 549,000 square miles, Portugal 825,000 square miles, Kongo Free State 905,000 square miles, the Boer Republics 178,000 square miles, which, with 2,435,000 square miles occupied by Morocco, Egypt, Sûdan, and Liberia, make about 11,000,000 square miles out of the entire 11,500,000 square miles said to be the superficial area of Africa.

It is from the above delimitations that we have to forecast the probable condition of Africa a hundred years hence.

Egypt's future depends largely upon the state she will be in when England retires from the care and control of her. For sixteen years England has been redeeming her from the anarchy she fell into through the wastefulness of Ismail the Khedive, the revolt of Arabi, and the rebellion of the Sûdan. During this period her finances have been restored and her army reorganised. The revenue has been steadily augmenting, her trade increased, the instituted reforms have tended to the happiness of her people; and now, assured of prosperity, she is advancing to regain her lost Sûdanese provinces. Last year the Egyptian troops were at Berber; this year they will be at Khartûm and Omdurman, and probably at the Bahr Ghazal. A couple of years hence Kordofan and Darfûr will have been occupied. Egypt must then devote several years — under British supervision — to the work of consolidation and restoration of these countries, which should occupy at least fifteen years more.

Despite assertions to the contrary, I do not think France will attempt forcibly to interfere with the British occupation until it is clear to all the world that Egypt is in a condition to conduct her own affairs. But notwithstanding the fact that the mutual action of England and Egypt may be comparatively smooth for fifteen or twenty years to come, the time must arrive when the new Egypt will be vehement in her desire to terminate the tutelage to which she will have submitted for nearly forty years. Then the good sense of England will perceive it necessary to withdraw the British troops. For the inestimable services she will have performed, England will doubtless demand the privileges of a protector, as security against relapse and the attempts of any foreign Power to succeed her.

For a few years after the departure of the British forces, the policy of the Egyptians will be cautious, and to proceed on the safe lines to which they will have been accustomed. Agriculture along the Upper Nile will be encouraged, Meroe will be developed, the Sûdan will be studded with fortified stations, and these will be connected by railways. If they continue this policy, enduring prosperity will be certain; but if a khedive of self-will seeks to restore the old order of things, override his councillors, veto legislative enactments, neglect the schools, overtax his people, then, of course, disaster and ruin must follow, and Egypt will once more need the foreigner to save her. I do not think it possible myself; on the contrary, the lessons of forty years will not be forgotten, and the end of the next century will find the Egyptian dominions thickly populated, independent of Turkey, protected by a powerful native army and ranking among the second-class Powers.

With regard to Abyssinia, I do not think the country will be much more advanced a hundred years hence than it is to-day, though a century is a long time to look forward to. A nation of mountaineers, so jealous of its independence and hostile to foreigners, cannot evolve out of itself the elements of progress in so short a period. The Abyssinians may possess breech-loaders, and have a better and larger army; but these in a barbarous nation rather tend to confirm its barbarism. They will be too powerful to be subdued, too dreaded for the attempt of a civiliser, too isolated to catch the spirit of civilisation, too poor to excite cupidity; in brief, the game of civilising Abyssinia is not worth the cost of the effort. More than once the Abyssinians will measure their strength against the Egyptians, and against the British to the south; but though they may meet with a temporary success, their defeat is assured in all the lowlands round about.

Italy claims African territory to the south of Abyssinia much too spacious for her revenue. Becoming infected with the craze for African territory and puffed up with vanity, she attempted to swallow more than she could digest. The result was satiety, and disgorgement. Her Somali and Galla lands, 280,000 square miles, are of no value to her, but are coveted by both France and Abyssinia. It is obvious to me that they will be a cause of trouble, expense, and humiliation to her yet. The sentiment against absentees is as strong with rival Powers as with private tenants. Italy, not daring the cost of proper occupation, must decide quickly what alternative she will adopt in regard to them. This section, then, being in a state of suspense, there is no certain basis for a forecast of the future. A few years hence it will be safer to pronounce it.

British East Africa has a fair future. In 1875 a traveller sounded the praises of Uganda, and suggested that it required missionaries. Two years later missionaries landed in the country, after a voyage across Lake Victoria. To-day there are 321 churches and over 100,000 converts in it. Parliament has voted £3,000,000 toward the railway which is to connect Uganda with the sea; 150 miles of it is now in running order. The terminus is to be on the shore of the lake, which will soon be floating many steam vessels. It will then be necessary to extend the railways, so as to make the frontiers of this region accessible and secure against disturbance. Lake Rudolf is one objective point which must be reached; Gondokoro on the White Nile is another; Lakes Albert Edward and Albert are others. By the time these necessary works are concluded, white communities will have established themselves along the trunk railway, the Kenia, Elgon, and Massowa mountains will possess their sanatoria and hotels, and long before the half of the century has gone British East Africa will have become one of the most prosperous African colonies, somewhat similar to what Natal is at present.

Under German Africa, I include East Africa, Damara, and Namaqua lands, and the Kamerun. Intellectually the native races of these countries are inferior to those of British East Africa, and the trend of German policy toward them does not promise great success. As against the constitutionalism of the British methods, it is a decided militarism that is in favour with the Germans ; and from such I gather that, successful as it may seem by steady persistence and force, only a kind of progress like that found in Boer States can follow. Military control permits no radical change among natives, and does not conduce to moral and intellectual improvement. Being too rigid and supercilious to stoop to associate with inferiors, it is satisfied with the outward form of civilisation. The tribes protected from mutual slaughter will naturally multiply, and supply labour for mines, public works, mercantile establishments, and agricultural estates; but, as there is no sign of elevating effort in view, the great mass of natives will not have profited morally by German civilisation. The German possession a century hence will be in much the same condition as the Gold Coast is to-day; that is, materially improved, but in heart and understanding only a degree above barbarism.

Portuguese East Africa, north of the Zambezi, has no remarkable future in prospect. Its climate and situation are against it. A certain improvement in government may be expected from pickings derived from trade passing by its borders to British Nyassaland. That part of the Portuguese possessions south of the Zambezi River is exposed to the demands of Rhodesia and the Transvaal; but as flexibility will be more advantageous than obduracy, and neither Boer nor British colonists will greatly care for malarious lowlands, the Portuguese will avert the danger by the freest access to the sea-posts of Beira and Lourenço Marquez, and thus render friction unlikely.

Neither Nyassaland nor northern Charterland, though in other ways prosperous enough, can present such results as British East Africa at the end of the next century, unless some sure curative of malarial fever is discovered. The tribes are a mere agglomeration of fragments of tribes, and though of the sturdier type, they are not intellectual. Before many years, education, which is freely bestowed, must necessarily make a great change in them. The connection of Lake Nyassa with the Cape must increase trade to a large extent, and otherwise be of material benefit. The rising importance of the Tanganyika region by the prosperity of the regions east and west of it, must be of great advantage to the revenue of Nyassaland; coffee, cotton, sugar, tea, etc., may be largely exported, and altogether the general progress may be most marked; still the area of Nyassaland is but limited, and northern Charterland is as yet in a primitive state, far in the interior, with nothing exceptionally promising. Should Rhodesia seek an outlet to the Atlantic at Mossamedes then Charterland's prospects would be brighter.

In treating of South Africa I must include Cape Colony, Natal, Bechuanaland, the South African Republic, and the Orange Free State, because want of space

forbids detail and compels brevity. The
most marked advance in Africa during the
next century will be in this region, because
it is suitable to the constitution of the
European, and for 250 years he has proved
himself adapted to it, and has already
founded several flourishing States within
it.   Even the youngest State is possessed
of all the advantages necessary to the
fullest expansion; railways, telegraphs,
and steam lines bring it in direct contact
with the centre of the civilised world.
Nevertheless, there is a peculiar condition
of things in South Africa, found in no
other part of the continent, which, as we
look forward along the coming century,
satisfy us that there must be a troublous
future in store for these colonies and States.
The worst danger, I think, to be appre-
hended is from the stubborn antagonism
which exists between two such determined
races as the British and the Dutch. Years
do not appear to modify, but rather to
intensify the incompatibility. Already
they have lived side by side under one
flag for over ninety years, but the feeling

has been more hostile of late years. The South African Bond (Boer) and the South African League (British) represent the variance of feeling existing. Though the Boers are in the majority at present, time appears to be in favour of the ultimate predominance of the British. During the last six years the steam lines took 66,000 people to South Africa, and Johannesburg, Kimberley, and Rhodesia must account for most of these. The next ten years at this rate will place the British as numerically equal to the Boers, and in twenty years they will exceed the Boers, and by that time the supremacy question will have been definitely settled.

The Imperial supremacy is an altogether different thing, and not worth considering. What we want to know is, if the supremacy is of such a character as to assure us of the largest possible civil and religious liberty to the people of South Africa. If the British are in the ascendant, the principles which triumphed in the United States, Canada, and the Australias will triumph here also; but if the Dutch gain

the ascendency, the outlook is not so
bright. In my opinion the latter can
scarcely be the case, though at present
Boer ideas and views preponderate. If a
happy solution of the problem be arrived
at, South Africa in 1998 must have
a population of European descent approaching 8,000,000 and a coloured population of 16,000,000. Sectional revolts of
blacks against whites will doubtless happen,
but any combination of the negroes of the
various States is impossible. Long before
the end of the century the connection of
South Africa with Great Britain will be
very slight, unless common interests will
have invented some form of nexus where-
by Britain and her colonies may have the
utmost freedom of action in domestic
matters, while yet restrained from pursu-
ing opposing politics in foreign affairs.

Portuguese Angola, which comes next,
possesses such advantages from its position and natural resources, as might, with
energetic administration, make it an opu-
lent colony. Its climate on the whole is
very tolerable for the tropics; it contains

spacious highlands, the soil of which is well adapted for cereals and grazing; in its valleys may be grown coffee, tea, cotton, sugar-cane, etc. It is rich in copper and iron. A judicious expenditure on railways would open out a rich interior, and enable it to share to a great extent in the prosperity of its neighbours. It possesses several good seaports which some day will attract the attention of North Charterland and Rhodesia. Mossamedes is but a thousand miles away from the Victoria Falls and less than 1,300 from Buluwayo, which fact is sufficiently suggestive of what the next century may see.

The existence of the Kongo Free State depends upon whether Belgium will succeed King Leopold in 1900. Hitherto she has been strongly disinclined to the idea. However, the completion of the Kongo Railway, which gives easy access to the Upper Kongo basin, may convert her to a better appreciation of the noble State the King has created. The shares are at present worth double their face value, the trade of the State is annually increasing, while the revenue may be made to keep pace with the expenditure at any time. The mortality due to climate shows a steady reduction, and by means of the railway, which will be open next June to regular traffic, and better accommodation on the river steamers, it will be still further reduced. In 1879 the ocean voyage to the Kongo occupied forty-five days; in 1898 the voyage takes twenty-two days; it will shortly pay to run steamers which will do the voyage in half the time. In thirteen years the number of Europeans on the Kongo has risen from a few score to 1,500; ten years hence, by the accelerated means of transport, I estimate there will be 5,000, and by 1998 there probably will be 250,000 Europeans within the State, and railways to the Tanganyika, the Nile, and Katanga. To-day the native population is estimated at 16,000,000, which a century hence will no doubt have increased to 40,000,000. But how easy it were to efface this fair prospect, by imagining the destiny of the State consigned to other hands than that of Belgium?

French Africa, which includes the Gabun, French Kongo, Dahomey, Senegal, Algiers, Tunis, the Sahara, and Nigeria, is too vast to be here treated of otherwise than under one head. Twice has France in the past possessed magnificent colonies; but during the wars of the Louises and Napoleon she has had the misfortune to lose them nearly all. She has acquired others since, as great and as valuable as those she lost; but Gallic nature remains the same as when Polybius declared the Gauls to be " swayed by impulse rather than by sober calculation." As in the far past the Gauls yielded to passion, were so needlessly provocative and prone to rash enterprises, it is to be feared that in the future they will not sufficiently deliberate upon the choice of evils, and so again endanger their vast possessions. Algiers, Tunis, and Senegal are, however, so well established that it is doubtful whether a calamitous war would interrupt their progress. But for the rest, unless a more prudent policy be adopted toward well-meaning nations, it is impossible to say what another century may bring forth. Like Italy, France has been forward in annexation; and her revenue is not equal to nourishing an Asian and an African empire of such prodigious extent and a huge island like Madagascar at one and the same time. One or the other must needs starve or all must suffer through the want of nutrition for development.

The British West African colonies during the coming century are destined to be much more progressive than in the past. Inclusive of Nigeria, their superficial area extends over 480,000 square miles. Hitherto they have been neglected and remained comparatively undeveloped; but owing to French aggressiveness, which threatened to limit them to the coast-line, they have of late received more attention, and railways have been started both at Lagos and Sierra Leone toward the interior. Cape Coast Castle is also to be connected with Kumassi. These lines will enable our merchants, so long confined to the coast, to enter into commercial relations with the more populous interior. To-day the revenue of these colonies amounts to £500,000, while their trade with that of Nigeria is valued at £6,000,000. Given a hundred years more, the trade will have increased to £25,000,000, while there will be a corresponding improvement in the social condition of the natives of these regions.

There remains only the Moroccan Empire to consider. Owing to the jealousies of the Powers, annexationists have been shy of Morocco. It must be the policy of Great Britain to uphold the native ruler as long as possible, were it only for the reason that if a foreign Power occupies Morocco, Gibraltar will have been flanked. It is certain that a course of British administration, similar to that which is regenerating Egypt, would have a decidedly beneficial effect on Morocco, and start it on a prosperous course. But this would not be done without the consent of Europe. Therefore, Morocco must be left to natural evolution which, of course, requires centuries to produce substantial civilisation. It is possible that some foreign Power will take advantage of some serious European entanglement to bring the Moroccan question to a sudden issue; but it will not be such an easy task as the seizure of Tunis, nor so quietly acquiesced in.

I have thus gone round Africa in a perfunctory way, I fear; still, if the reader will take the map of the continent in hand and study the limits I have given in each paragraph he will find the sum total of the changes, which the next century must see, to be very large. The Cape to Cairo Railway, which some appear to think as improbable, will be an accomplished fact before 1925, I believe. There is nothing very difficult about it, for even to-day £10,000,000 would rail the entire distance from Buluwayo to Lado on the White Nile; and with steam navigation on Lakes Nyassa, Tanganyika, Albert Edward, and Albert, and on the White Nile, communication would be established between Cape Town and Alexandria.

THE PARTITION OF AFRICA.

THE PARTITION OF AFRICA.

BY J. SCOTT KELTIE, LL.D.,

Secretary of the Royal Geographical Society.

FOURTEEN years ago I wrote a paper entitled " The Scramble for Africa." In the beginning of 1884 that scramble had just begun. Up to that time England and France were the two great European Powers in Africa; but they pursued their annexations leisurely. Portugal, though she possessed some 800,000 square miles in East and West Africa, was hardly taken into account, and in the scramble was dealt with by the other Powers as if she were a native State. The King of the Belgians was pushing his way on the Kongo rather as the head of a private company than as the sovereign of a State; France was fighting her way toward the Upper Niger, while the British Niger Company was establishing its footing on the lower river. Even British

South Africa did not, fourteen years ago,
extend much beyond the Orange River;
and over the whole of Central Africa,
i. e., Africa between the tropics, effective
European possession was confined to a
few patches along the coast. Suddenly
Germany intervened, and precipitated the
leisurely game of annexation into a scramble. In 1883 the German flag was raised
by a private trader on the coast of Namaqualand, in Southwest Africa. In 1884 the
scramble began in earnest; and by 1885
the "Spheres" of the three great European Powers chiefly interested — England,
France, and Germany — may be said to
have been roughly blocked out over the
whole continent. Meantime, in 1884–85,
the Berlin Congress had met and laid
down the rules for the game, at the same
time recognising the Kongo Free State
under the sovereignty of the Belgians.
During the years that have elapsed since
then there have been occasional crises
among the Powers concerned when their
African frontiers approached each other;
but till now the difficulty has been got

over by international agreements. There
was so much elbow-room on the great
neglected continent that mutually satisfactory arrangements were not difficult.
But now that the continent has been practically partitioned, and the various spheres
delimited, the Powers have been taking
stock of the extent and value of their
possessions, and one, at least, is not satisfied. Let us briefly inquire what the
result has been.

British South Africa now extends from
Cape Town to Lake Tanganyika, a distance of 1,800 miles. The whole south
coast is British. On the west the sphere
is bordered by German Southwest Africa,
Portuguese Guinea, and the Kongo Free
State; on the east by Portuguese and
German East Africa, while the two Boer
Republics are shut into the British spheres
as inclosures. It may be said that the
only disputed boundary in this part of
Africa is between Great Britain and
Portugal, the Barotse country to the west
of the Zambezi being claimed by both;
the difference will probably be settled in

favour of the stronger Power. This immense British area, covering nearly a
million of square miles, is at various stages
of incorporation with the Empire, from the
self-administrating colony to the " Sphere
of Influence "; Cape Colony and Natal
belong to the former categories. Beyond
Cape Colony we have the Bechuanaland
Protectorate, but much the greater share
belongs to the British South African
Company, whose territories extend to the
heart of the continent. On the west and
south of Lake Nyassa we have the British
Central Africa Protectorate, which is under
direct imperial administration and is independent of the company. A traveller
from the Cape to Lake Tanganyika might
sail up the lake and from the north end,
after a journey of about 120 miles either
through the Kongo Free State or through
German East Africa, find himself again in
British territory, in the country of which we
have recently heard so much, — Uganda.
Here we are in British East Africa, which
has a coast-line on the Indian Ocean of
some 400 miles to the south of the Juba

River, extends westward to the Victoria Nyanza, the Albert Nyanza, and the Albert Edward Nyanza, and on the other side along the Juba, and westward across the Nile into Bahr-el-Ghazal and Darfûr. It includes the islands of Zanzibar and Pemba, and embraces an area of some 800,000 square miles. The limits of British East Africa have been arranged by agreements with Germany and Italy, the two contiguous Powers; but they have never been formally recognised by France — and thereby hangs a tale to which we shall presently refer. This vast territory is under the jurisdiction nominally of Her Majesty's representative at Zanzibar, but it is divided into provinces each with its resident and sub-residents, though the portion to the north of Uganda on the Upper Nile has not yet been finally occupied. The island of Zanzibar has still a Sultan as nominal ruler; but he is a mere figure-head. On the northeast, British East Africa is bordered by Somaliland and Gallaland, which is nominally Italian, except a block on the Gulf of

Aden to the west of Cape Guardafui, which is British. It covers 75,000 square miles, and it is of great importance as commanding the trade of the interior.

On the opposite side of Africa will be found another extensive British sphere covering the lower Niger. The total area secured by various agreements between England, France, and Germany, and by treaties with native potentates is about 500,000 square miles ; all except a portion on the coast, which is a protectorate, being under the jurisdiction of the Royal Niger Company. About the eastern boundary there is no dispute; it extends from the south end of Lake Tchad in a southwest direction to the coast near the Calabar River. On the north, by arrangement with France in 1890, the British territory is bordered by a line drawn from Say on the Niger east to Barua on Lake Tchad, but bending northward so as to include all that belongs to Sokoto. It is the western boundary that is at present in hot dispute between France and England. The English in-

terpretation of the agreement of 1890 is
that a line drawn south from Say marks
the western boundary of the British
sphere; and this was the French interpretation when the agreement was made.
The Niger Company has made treaties
with native chiefs so as to cover all this
sphere. For reasons satisfactory to the
company they have not occupied every
point in this territory, among others the
important town of Busa on the Niger.
The French maintaining, by an erroneous
interpretation of the Berlin Agreement,
that effective occupation is necessary,
have slipped in and occupied Busa and
other places. The fact is, it is only now,
when the partition is all but complete,
that France realises her disadvantage in
having no direct access to the Lower
Niger. Great Britain has apparently
made up her mind on no account to yield
any part of the west bank of the Lower
Niger to France, except a small strip to
the south of Say. France insists on her
rights as actual occupant. The two
Powers are, therefore, at a deadlock; what

the result will be remains to be seen.[1]
These British Niger territories are the
most densely peopled part of Africa; they
are capable of great commercial development; many of the people are far above
the rank of savages. Lagos, the Gold
Coast, Sierra Leone, Gambia, all British,
have been reduced to patches blocked
everywhere from the interior by French
territory, except Lagos, which is really
part of the great Niger territory and
which, along with this and the Niger
Coast Protectorate, will shortly be united
under one administration under direct
Imperial control. The total area in Africa
claimed by Great Britain may be roughly
estimated at 2,300,000 square miles.

The territory claimed by France in
Africa covers something like three million square miles, including Madagascar.
Algeria and Tunis she holds by right of
conquest, and her claims there are not
disputed.   From the Mediterranean to

[1] By a compact announced in the Speech from the Throne,
August 12th, 1898, the deadlock mentioned here has been
broken.   The French have abandoned their claim to Busa, receiving in return some minor territorial concessions. The result
must be viewed as a diplomatic victory for England. — H. T. P.

the Gulf of Guinea her territory extends without interruption. By the Anglo-French arrangement of 1890, already referred to, the greater part of the Sahara, " very light soil," as Lord Salisbury called it, is allotted as her sphere. On the northwest she is shut off from the coast by Morocco and the Spanish block known as Rio d'Oro, about 150,000 square miles. From a little to the north of Cape Blanco round to the British Gold Coast Colony, France possesses a long line of coast, interrupted by such patches as British Gambia, Portuguese Guinea, Liberia, and Sierra Leone. The whole of the Niger above Say is French, and nearly the whole of the country in the great bend of the river is claimed by her; and, as a matter of fact, the disputed area is very small. It consists of a patch behind the British Gold Coast and German Togoland, mainly composed of the Kingdom of Mossi. Great Britain claims some of the territory behind Ashanti, and within the last few months France and Germany have come to an agreement as to the limits of Togoland. The whole region to the west of this, included in the basins of the Niger and the Senegal, are French and all the territory embraced in the northern bend of the Niger. This is known as the French Sûdan, with the exception of the most westerly portions, Senegambia. Like the Niger territories, this region is densely populated and capable of great commercial development. The French Sahara probably covers 1,500,000 square miles, and Senegambia and the French Sûdan close on half a million square miles.

Further south, on the equator, the French Kongo extends from the coast along the north side of the Kongo River, north to Lake Tchad, and east to the water — parting between the Nile and the Kongo. These limits, by arrangements between France, Germany, and the Kongo Free State, are beyond dispute. They include an area of some 560,000 square miles; but France is not satisfied with this. She declines to accept the eastern boundary, and during the last five years has been making strenuous efforts to extend her sphere into the Bahr-el-Ghazal district, — one of the abandoned provinces of the Egyptian Sûdan, and included in British East Africa, in accordance with the agreement between Great Britain, Germany, and Italy. These agreements, France declares, are not binding upon her; and at the present moment the relations between France and England are in a state of tension, because an expedition, under Captain Marchand, is reported actually to have reached the Nile, and established itself at Fashoda, while another French expedition from Abyssinia has completed, or is endeavouring to complete the French connection between the West and East Coasts. Some three years ago it was declared in the House of Commons that any attempt on the part of France to establish herself on the Nile would be regarded as "an unfriendly act." It is here, then, and on the Niger, that the final crisis in the partition of Africa has been reached. The eagerness of France to find a footing on the Upper Nile is intimately associated

with the position of England in Egypt,
which, as all the world knows, is bitterly
resented by the French. Egypt is nominally under the suzerainty of Turkey, but
is practically independent, or, rather, under
the tutelage of England. Under the guidance of England, an attempt, so far successful, is being made to regain the lost
provinces of the Egyptian Sûdan, so long
terrorised by the Khalifa. An advance
has been made to within measurable distance of Khartûm; if that stronghold
should be taken, it would mean the defeat
of the Khalifa. Doubtless no time would
be lost in establishing an Anglo-Egyptian
rule in the old provinces, Kordofan, Darfûr, and Bahr-el-Ghazal. If the French
are found to be actually established in the
last-named province, and if no compro-
mise can be come to, then a crisis will
have been reached which will affect not
only the partition of Africa, but the peace
of the world. These Egyptian Sûdan
provinces cover an area of some 800,000
square miles, while that of Egypt proper,
from the Desert to the Red Sea, is about

400,000 square miles. To the west of
Egypt is the Turkish territory of Tripoli
and Fezzan, to the south of which is a
portion of the Sahara, at present unannexed, and, with the exception of the
Tibesti Highlands, a hopeless desert.
This unannexed area probably covers
about 800,000 square miles; on its southern border is the semi-civilised Sûdan
State of Wadai, at present independent,
but which ultimately, no doubt, will be
claimed by France.

Just at the mouth of the Red Sea,
opposite Aden, France has a block of
territory, Obok, estimated to cover 50,000
square miles, its only value being that
it commands Abyssinia. Partly by conquest and partly by international arrangement, France is in undisputed possession
of Madagascar, which with neighbouring
islands covers an area of about 280,000
square miles. Altogether, then, the ac-
knowledged claims of France in Africa
gives her the enormous area of about
3,300,000 square miles, much of it sand.

Germany, which may be said to have

begun the scramble, came off with an area much less than the other two Powers. However, unlike the others, she began fifteen years ago with nothing, and now has undisputed possession of about a million square miles. In Southwest Africa, where she began her acquisitions, her possessions — Damaraland and Namaqualand — by arrangement with England, cover 322,450 square miles. Except in the north, it is doubtful if this half-desert country can ever be of much value. Germany's greatest African territory is in East Africa, marching with British East Africa in the north and with Portuguese East Africa and British Central Africa on the south. It includes the southern half of the Victoria Nyanza and the eastern shore of Tanganyika. It has about 400 miles of coast-line. The possession is undisputed, based on arrangements with England and Portugal, Zanzibar and native chiefs in 1885–90. It only remains to settle a few details with England as to the southern boundary. Attempts with varied success have been made to establish plantations in the north of the territory; but at present the bulk of the country is untouched, and much of it is just a stage beyond desert; it covers 385,000 square miles. On the opposite coast, between French Kongo and the British Niger territory, Germany possesses an area of over 190,000 square miles in the Kamerun, which extends eastward into the interior some 400 miles and north through Adamawa to Lake Tchad. By arrangement with Great Britain and France the limits of the German concessions are practically settled, and the country, which is thickly populated, is in a fair state of development. German Togoland is a long, narrow strip on the Gold Coast. By an agreement with France in 1897, its limits as respects French Dahomey have been settled, and the colony may now cover about 25,000 square miles.

But to the west of this and to the north of Ashanti is a neutral zone as between Germany and England, which remains to be adjusted. About this there is not likely to be much difficulty; and it is not probable that unless through some cataclysm or cession by the other Powers the German area in Africa will ever exceed the million square miles.

When the scramble began, Portugal put in enormous claims for an "empire" across the continent between Angola and Mozambique. This was made short work of by England and the Kongo Free State; and her possessions have been restricted to a long strip on the East Coast, with a wedge along the Zambezi, and a much bigger block on the West Coast between the rivers Cunene and Kongo. The actual jurisdiction of the Portuguese, especially on the east, hardly extends beyond the coast. In Portuguese West Africa, as has already been pointed out, the region to the west of the Upper Zambezi is claimed by the British South African Company; meantime a provincial agreement exists pending the final settlement. On the Guinea coast all that remains of Portugal's old possessions is a small strip of 14,000 square miles south of the Gambia; she also retains the Cape

Verde Islands and St. Thomas. Altogether the African possessions of Portugal cover only 750,000 square miles.

The Kongo Free State, which practically coincides with the enormous basin of the river Kongo, is the creation of the Berlin Congress of 1884–85. Its boundaries are defined by international agreements with the leading Powers concerned, dating from 1884 to 1894. It covers 900,000 square miles, and has a population of, probably, 30,000,000 native Africans. By a convention with Great Britain in 1894, a strip along the west of the Albert Nyanza and the Upper Nile was leased to the King of the Belgians. This strip extended much further than it at present does; but, under pressure from France, the King gave up the northern section. The Kongo Free State possesses the most magnificent series of waterways on the continent.

There is only one other Power largely interested in Africa, though that interest has been lately largely diminished. Italy could not resist the example of the other great Powers. She had long had an eye on Tripoli, but France virtually warned her to keep her hands off that. So long ago as 1870 an Italian trading house had obtained the cession of a spot of territory on Assab Bay, near the mouth of the Red Sea, as a coaling station. In 1882 Italy took active possession of this spot, and in 1883 she began to extend her territory northward until in 1888 she reached Cape Kasar, north of the port of Massaua, 650 miles north of Assab. Had Italy been content with this strip, and used it as a basis of commercial operations with Abyssinia, all might have gone well. But she was ambitious far beyond the limit of her means. She would needs conquer Abyssinia. Space prevents us entering into details. Suffice it to say that, after long-continued operations, Italy met with disastrous defeat, and is now confined to the limits of her strip on the Red Sea, about 88,500 square miles, and Abyssinia has asserted its independence. But she was not content with Abyssinia. By various concessions Italy obtained a

footing in Somaliland, to the north of the
river Juba, and claimed an area here of
335,000 square miles. She has not formally renounced this, but as a matter of
fact she must give it up. At present, with
the aid of the French Prince Henry of
Orleans and the Russian Colonel Leon-
tieff, Abyssinia is preparing to sweep the
whole of Somaliland and Gallaland within
her grasp ; and it is stated that England
has even consented to give up more than
half her territory on the Gulf of Aden.
At present, then, Italy's effective claim
is limited to the area of Eritrea, as her
Red Sea strip is named.

Besides the block, Rio d'Oro, already
referred to, on the Sahara coast, Spain
possesses the Canaries, Tetuan in Morocco, Fernando Po, and one or two other
islands, and a patch on the Guinea coast,
— altogether about 3,800 square miles.
Liberia, the negro Republic, is still nominally independent, though France has cut
down her territory to 14,600 square miles.
Through the jealousy of the several Powers
interested — Spain, France, Germany, and

England — Morocco still remains unannexed, though it is to be hoped, for the sake of its wretched inhabitants, that that will not be for long; it covers an area of 220,000 square miles.

The general result of our examination of the partition of Africa may be summarised briefly in the following table, in which an approximate estimate is given of the area claimed by the different European Powers and that which may still be regarded as independent:

	Square miles.
France	3,300,000
Great Britain	2,300,000
Germany	925,000
Kongo Free State	900,000
Portugal	750,000
Italy (including Somaliland) . . .	420,000
Spain	214,000
Boer Republics	168,000
Abyssinia	195,000
Morocco	220,000
Liberia	14,600
Turkey (Egypt [1] and Tripoli) . . .	800,000
Mahdi's territories	650,000
Wadai	150,000
Unannexed Sahara	800,000
Lakes	68,000
Total Africa	11,874,600

[1] Including regained territories on the Upper Nile.

At present these are little more than figures. It has been pointed out that the final crisis in the partition of Africa lies between France and Great Britain on the Niger and on the Nile. Whether the one succeeds or the other, in gaining its point, will not materially affect the figures in the above table; but the result may have a very important bearing on the commercial and social development of the continent. It is not my business in this article to discuss the value of the various areas claimed by the different Powers; but, in conclusion, I may be allowed to point out one interesting fact. In the whole of Africa's nearly twelve million odd square miles there are probably not more than 1,200,000 whites to 150,000,000 natives. Of the former 750,000 are in Africa, south of the Zambezi, and over 300,000 in Algeria and Tunis, leaving 150,000 for all the rest of the continent. South Africa is the one section of the continent which may become the home of generations of Europeans, and in this respect England has fared best of all the Powers. Of the continent between the tropics, all experience up to the present goes to show that it can never be colonised by white races, but must be developed by the natives under white supervision.

THE BRITISH EMPIRE
IN AFRICA.

THE BRITISH EMPIRE IN AFRICA.

BY W. T. STEAD.

Editor of the " Review of Reviews."

LESS than forty years ago it was a commonly received doctrine among British statesmen that Africa was worthless. A select Committee of the House of Commons, in the early sixties, reported that the settlements on the West Coast of Africa cost more than they were worth, and recommended the gradual abandonment of the country. Even in the seventies there were eminent men who argued earnestly in favour of the abandonment of the whole of South Africa, with the exception of a coaling station at the Cape of Good Hope. But a change came o'er the spirit of the British dream when, in the early eighties, they saw all the nations of Europe prepare to take part in a passionate scramble for the Dark Continent. That which they despised and wished to

4

throw away in the sixties, became in the
nineties the coveted objects of Imperial
ambition. Now, when the century is
closing, the pick of the continent is
coloured British Red.

British Africa can be variously described, — geographically, politically, eth-
nologically, and religiously. But the
simplest definition is this, all Africa that
is comfortably habitable by white men is
under the British flag or under British
protection. And again, everything in
Africa that pays dividends lies within the
sphere pegged out for John Bull by his
adventurous sons. Wherever in Africa
you find land in which white-skinned
children can be bred and reared, you will
find it lies within the British zone. And
wherever there is in Africa any paying
property, that also will be found to be
within the same sphere of influence. All
of Africa that is habitable and all of
Africa that pays its way, that is British
Africa.

The other nations have scrambled for
John Bull's leavings. France, for in-

stance, has annexed the Sahara. In her
West African colony of Senegal every
fifth European is a French official. Germany has annexed 320,000 square miles of
desert in the southwest, and 400,000 of
semi-tropical land in the east; but they
have more officials than colonists, more
subsidies than dividends. Portugal has
quite an empire of malarial marshes on
both coasts. Belgium has the Kongo
Free State, a magnificent empire in the
heart of tropical Africa which needs
£80,000 a year subsidy from Belgium to
keep it from bankruptcy, and which, notwithstanding the subsidy, has run up a
debt of over £8,000,000. Italy, the last to
join in the scramble, has nearly come to
grief over her African adventure. Africa
stands solely on the debit side of the account of every European nation but one,
and even in the case of Britain the entries
to the bad are neither few nor small.

British Africa may be described in another way. Wherever you find a good
harbour in Africa or a navigable river or a
great inland lake, there you may be sure

the British flag is not far off.   The Kongo
is the only great African river which does
not enter the sea under British protection.
The Kongo was opened up, "boomed,"
and made accessible by Mr. Stanley, a
British explorer; and its waters are as
free to the flags of all nations as if they
were British.   The only harbour in Southern Africa that is worth having which is
not British is Delagoa Bay, and John Bull
to this day ruefully recalls the fact that he
only lost that by allowing it to be sent
to arbitration before a tribunal which took
more account of musty little deeds of a
remote past than the necessities of the living present.   The only harbour on the
southwest coast, the natural port of German Southwest Africa, is Walfisch Bay,
where a British sentry stands on guard
under the shade of the Union Jack.
Wherever navigable water is, there the
descendant of the old Vikings recognises
his Fatherland even in the heart of Africa.
Of the great lakes which lie in a long
string from the Zambezi to the Nile, there
is not one on whose shores there is not

a British possession. Even the smaller lakes, such as Lake Tchad, seem to attract the sea-rovers of the Northland.

There is less objection taken by the other Powers to this extraordinary monopoly of the ocean gates of a continent, because no other Power believes that its interests demand that it should admit all the world to its markets on equal terms with its own subjects. The British may be right, or they may be wrong. They make no claim to superiority of altruism to their neighbours. Their policy is undoubtedly prompted by self-interest; but British self-interest takes the form of opening all British possessions freely to the traders of the world, whereas the self-interest of other nations leads them to impose differential and prohibitive duties upon the goods of foreign competitors. It is not surprising that the second vote of all the nations is given to Britain. So rigorously is this rule enforced that the Imperial Government ruthlessly rejected the proposals made by Mr. Rhodes, which tended, in the remote future, to the imposition of heavier duties on foreign than on British-made goods. Britain has now occupied Egypt for fifteen years, but so far has she abused her opportunity to close the Egyptian market upon her rivals that the comparative volume of British trade to that of other nations is less to-day than it was before the country was occupied.

Another reason why British rule has spread so rapidly is because England alone among the nations carried to Africa the principle of religious liberty conjoined with religious propaganda. British Africa is the product of three forces, — British conquest, British trade, and British missions. And of the three the first counts for the least, and the last for the greatest factor in expansion of Britain in Africa. The Roman Catholic priests sent out by the Portuguese in olden days were zealous but intolerant. The Roman Catholic priests sent out by the Freethinking French Republic have only recently arrived on the field. The few German and Swiss missionaries have been too few to leave much mark on the continent. But

British missionaries have been everywhere the pioneers of empire. The British frontier has advanced on the stepping-stones of missionary graves. Deduct the missionary from the sum total of the forces which have coloured the African map red from Table Mountain to the Zambezi, and the Empire disappears. It was David Moffat, the missionary, who led the way into Central Africa from the south. It was his dauntless son-in-law, the missionary Livingstone, who pierced the heart of the Dark Continent in which he laid down his life; and it was Moffat's successor, the missionary Mackenzie, who secured the open road from the Cape to the Zambezi along which Cecil Rhodes subsequently marched to empire.

It is true that Britain did not first go to Africa to convert the heathen. It is a melancholy fact that her first relations with the African continent were those connected with the slave-trade. The West Coast was, in the sixteenth century, the great emporium of the traffic in human beings. The first form of the scramble for

Africa took the shape of a keen competition among the sea-faring nations for the profitable business of buying negroes cheap in the Gulf of Guinea, and selling them dear in the West Indies and in the Southern States. The slave-trade began in Elizabeth's reign. It was not finally extirpated till our century. On the whole, the ships of Europe are estimated to have transported ten million Africans to the American continent. Europe was the middleman in this traffic of the continents. Africa sold, America bought. It was a rude system of emigration by which the overflow of the Old World was discharged upon the New. Of the 100,000 dusky and involuntary emigrants who were transported across the Atlantic every year, about 30,000 sailed under the British flag. Britain, like the other nations, had her foot planted on the West African coast, not to colonise but to buy slaves. The first European settlements were little more than the African counterpart of Castle Garden, — barracoons where the expatriated ones from the interior were

mustered before their shipment to their
ultimate destination. As wars were fre-
quent in those days, and every man had
more or less to fight for his own band, the
French, the Dutch, the Portuguese, and
the British studded the coast with forts, a
few of which still remain, although their
original use has long since disappeared.
After the slave-trade was suppressed in
1808, the prosperity of the Guinea Coast
dwindled, and it was many years before
the trade in gin and other alcoholic drinks
revived the fortunes of the West African
merchants. Then the scramble for markets recommenced. The Germans, who
manufacture the cheapest intoxicant, entered the field. The soldier came to the
rescue of the trader. Britain twice sent
an armed force to dictate terms in the
capital of Ashanti. The French crushed
Dahomey, despite the army of Amazons,
and bickering about the respective limits
of the hinterlands of the three Powers
has been going on ever since.

In West Africa the British possessions
are none of them colonies in the sense of

being territories in which Britons settle
and found families to rear up new nations.
The climate forbids that. The only white
men on the coast are officials, traders, and
missionaries. Sierra Leone, long known
as the White Man's Grave, was but typi-
cal of the whole of the group of West
African possessions. These possessions
may be thus described.

1. The Gambia, a Crown colony, governed by an administrator appointed by
the Colonial Office in London, is chiefly
notable because it commands the mouth
of the river Gambia, the only West
African river navigable by ocean-going
steamers. Its exports consist almost entirely of ground-nuts, which are crushed
for their oil in France; its imports, gunpowder, gin, cotton, and sugar. Population, 13,000; revenue, £25,000; exports
and imports, £225,000. First discovered
by the Portuguese; founded by the British
in 1686.

2. Sierra Leone was ceded to Britain in
1787 by the native chief, to form an asy-
lum for destitute negroes in England. It

was, therefore, a colony proper, founded to receive emigrants. Many liberated slaves were settled there. The colony stretches along 180 miles of coast-line. Its trade consists of exchanging palm-oil and palm kernels for hardware, cotton, gunpowder, tobacco, and spirits, — a Crown colony, with governor appointed by the Crown. Revenue, £110,000; exports and imports, £940,000. Attached to the colony there is a protectorate over about 20,000 miles in the neighbourhood.

3. The Gold Coast stretches about 250 miles along the coast, and extends some 300 miles into the interior, with an indefinite hinterland. It was first founded by a chartered company; the settlements were transferred to the Crown in 1821. In 1874 they were constituted a separate colony, with a governor appointed by the Crown. Population, 1,500,000, of whom 150 are Europeans; revenue, £240,000; imports and exports, £1,570,000; exports, gold, ivory, copal, palm-oil, rubber; imports, cotton, alcohol, and hardware.

4. Lagos, like Sierra Leone, is a colony

and a protectorate. It was the headquarters of the slave-trade. Then it became a great missionary centre. In 1861 it was taken over by Britain, and in 1886 was established as a separate colony, with a governor of its own. Exports, palm-oil and kernels, and imports, chiefly cotton goods (£270,000), spirits (£106,000), and tobacco (£25,000). Population, 2,000,000; revenue, £140,000; exports and imports, £1,900,000.

5. The Niger Coast Protectorate covers the whole coast from Lagos to the German possessions in the Kameruns, except the mouth of the Niger. Governed by a Royal Commissioner. Protectorate established in 1885. Recently its authority was carried farther inland by an expedition which suppressed human sacrifices in Benin city. Exports, palm-oil, kernels, rubber, ebony, and ivory; imports, cotton, cutlery, and coopers' stores. Revenue, £150,000; imports and exports, £1,600,000.

6. The Royal Niger Company. This chartered company, with a capital of

£1,100,000, has established the most
prosperous of all the West African colonies. It is practically sovereign over the
whole of the Lower and Middle Niger.
It has its own army and fleet. It makes
treaties, levies war, conquers territory,
suppresses the slave-trade, and, in short,
exercises sovereign authority over the
wealthiest and most populous region in
all Central Africa. The Niger Company
is much more rigorous in restricting the
sale of rifles and of spirits into its possessions than any other British colony.
North of latitude 7, all import of spirits
is interdicted, and elsewhere so high a
duty has been charged that the import of
rum and gin has dwindled to one-fourth
what it was before the charter was
granted. Exports, rubber, palm-oil, ivory,
guns, and hides; imports, cotton, woollens,
silks, hardware, salt, and earthenware. The
chief man is Sir George Taubman Goldie,
the Cecil Rhodes of West Africa, a quiet,
determined little man, with a genius for
government, whose word is law among
30,000,000 of Africans, and who, when

that word is not obeyed, teaches the diso-
bedient with Maxim guns that the way of
the transgressor is *hard.*

When we pass from West Africa to
East Africa, we come to a totally different
class of possessions. Properly speaking,
Britain possesses nothing in East Africa.
All that is British on the East Coast, until
you come to Zululand, is denominated
Protectorate. In a protectorate there is less
direct government by Britain. In a Crown
colony the laws are made and administered
by the Government. In a protectorate
the British undertake to protect the native authorities from foreign attack, to put
down the slave-trade, to restrain internecine war, to open up trade routes, to
maintain a kind of Roman peace; but
otherwise the inhabitants are left very
much to do as they please. Protectorates are looked after by commissioners
who are also Consuls-General. They are
appointed by the Crown. British domination in East Africa began in our own
times. For half a century and more the
natives of India crossing the sea had estab-

lished themselves in business largely as money-lenders in Zanzibar. But no European Power had planted its foot on the equatorial East. In 1888, however, thanks chiefly to the enterprise of a Scotchman, the Imperial British East Africa Company was formed and incorporated by Royal Charter. It received permission to accept a lease, to administer territories lying between the Indian Ocean and the great equatorial lakes. This chartered company never paid. "You cannot run a fort on coffee planting," said Mr. Rhodes. "Gold or diamonds can do it — nothing else." So after a time the company was wound up, receiving £250,000 for its assets, and the task of administering its million square miles was undertaken by the Imperial fort. This was in 1895. Its sphere of influence was then divided up into the following protectorates:

1. The East African, capital Mombasa, the finest harbour on the East Coast.

2. Uganda, the pearl of Africa, discovered by Mr. Stanley, snatched by Captain Lugard from the hands of the French, and

now in the throes of a mutiny, is the cock-
pit of Central Africa.   Heathens, Protestants, and Catholics are always struggling
for the mastery.   It is the land of romance
and of the unexpected.   It commands the
northern shores of the Victoria Nyanza
and the head waters of the Nile.

3. The Witu Protectorate is a small
tract of land governed by a Sultan, with a
British Resident, at the mouth of the river
Tana.

4. Zanzibar, the great commercial en-
trepot of Eastern Africa.   Population of
the island, 250,000.   Exports and imports
of the port, not including trans-shipments
in harbour, £ 2,400,100 per annum.   Governed by a Sultan, under a British Commissioner, since 1890.

5. Nyassaland.   This is now called the
British Central Africa Protectorate.   It is
an appendage to Lake Nyassa.   It is approached by the Zambezi, and is notable
as the seat of the Blantyre mission station,
as a thriving coffee plantation, and as a
scene of almost continual warfare against
the slave-traders.

Of all the regions now administered by the British, those of East Africa supply most elements of adventure and of romance. There we see white men from the Northern European seas, using the fighting men of Northern India in order to establish a Roman peace among the black races of Central Africa. Europe uses Asia as her sword to civilise Africa. These regions are continually witnessing scenes that recall the adventures of Ivanhoe or the warlike prowess of the Lion Heart; but the Knights Templar of to-day wear white felt helmets and use Maxims, steamboats, locomotive engines, and the printing-press as their instruments of conquest. On Lake Nyassa there are two gunboats, and in East Africa the British Government is spending three million sterling in constructing a railway 600 miles long, which will place the seaboard in direct railway communication with the heart of Central Africa. Three thousand coolies have been employed on the line since January, 1896, and the rate of construction is now said to be about half a mile a day.

66   The British Empire

We now come to the most important section of British Africa, that which lies at the southern extremity of the great continent.   It is only in this southern section that the British race is founding colonies properly so called.   In the lofty plateaux of Southern Africa the climate is so delightful that the country is becoming the sanatorium of the Empire.   Mr. Cecil Rhodes himself was first sent out to the Cape in the forlorn hope that South Africa might enable him to throw off the consumption that appeared to have seated itself on his lungs.   Olive Schreiner declares that after one has breathed the air of the Karoo, the air anywhere else seems thick and heavy.   There is champagne in its atmosphere.   It is not only the climate that is attractive.   South Africa has been for the past twenty years the great El Dorado of the world.   No other continent has ever produced within such narrow limits such a Golconda as the diamond mines of De Beers, such a storehouse of gold as the Rand of Johannesburg.   Out of the blue clay at Kimberley there have been dug, in the last twenty years, diamonds which have been sold for £70,000,000. Out of the Reef below Johannesburg gold has been brought to bank of the value of £50,000,000. The annual output is approaching £10,000,000, and before the Rand is exhausted it is calculated gold valued at £450,000,000 will be brought to bank. Behind the Diamond Fields and golden Johannesburg lies the land of Ophir of Rhodesia where, as yet, mining operations have only just begun. Greater, however, than diamonds and more valuable than gold is the master of diamonds and of gold. South Africa is chiefly famous as the pedestal of Cecil Rhodes, the most conspicuous and commanding personality which the British colonies have produced in our generation. The limits of space allotted to these articles render it impossible to describe, except in the briefest detail, the great divisions of Residential Africa. But before entering upon the detail of the provinces it is necessary to say a word as to the general location of the whole. South Africa is all British

with the exception of the German protectorate over the desert region in the southwest, and the narrow strip of Portuguese
territory that cuts off the Transvaal and
Rhodesia from the sea.   The Germans
have no port.   The Portuguese have
two, — Beira and Lourenço Marquez on
Delagoa Bay.   With these exceptions all
South Africa, from the Cape to far to the
north of the Zambezi, lies under the shel-
tering protection of the British flag.
Within the British influence are the two
Boer Republics of the Transvaal and the
Orange Free State.   These republics are
absolutely free from any interference in
their internal affairs from without.   They
have the protection without the taxation
or the authority of the Empire.   Sooner
or later they will abandon their attitude
of isolation and unite with the colonies
by which they are surrounded.   As Mr.
Rhodes recently declared : " Although we
human atoms may divide this country,
nature does not.   Nature does not and
the Almighty does not.   Whether in
Cape Town, in Durban, or in Rho-

desia, the interests are the same. The languages are the same. Those who form these States are the same, connected in their family and domestic relations and the like; and any one who tries to separate them in that feeling and action is doing an impossible thing." South Africa one and indivisible from Table Mountain to the great Equatorial lakes is the idea of Cecil Rhodes; and when Cecil Rhodes thinks, thoughts are things.

The premier colony in South Africa, that of the Cape, has now extended itself so far up-country that its title is a misnomer. Originally discovered by the Portuguese, it was first colonised by the Dutch in 1652. For a hundred years it was little more than a naval station, with a back country useful for the settlement, where native labour was plentiful and native land could be had, if not for the asking, then for the shooting. When the French Revolutionary wars broke out, the exiled Prince of Orange made over the Cape to the British, who promptly took possession in 1796. They gave it back, however, at the Peace of Amiens, in 1803; but when war broke out again it was recaptured by the British, in 1806, and it has never since passed out of their possession. The Dutch to this day are in a majority of the agricultural population, not only in the Boer Republics, but in the Cape Colony itself. When the British came, their ideas as to the rights of slaves to freedom offended the conservative Boers, who trekked northward to lands where the divine right of slavery was not interfered with, and the meddling Britishers would not be able to interfere with their peculiar institution. But many of the Dutch remained behind, and to this day the farming interest in the Cape is substantially Dutch. The natives were tolerably thick on the ground at first; but the coming of the white men thinned them off. The Hottentots and Bushmen are vanishing like the Maori and the Australian aborigines. Far different was the case of the Kaffir, the sturdy child of the great Bantu race. In him the white man, whether Dutch or British, has encountered a man as vigorous as himself. The Bantu is not dying out. He is increasing and multiplying and replenishing South Africa. The black and white races are flourishing side by side, and the great question of the future is, how their mutual multiplication may be so ordered as to leave room for both. Cape Colony has been continually extending its frontiers northward.

For a long time it halted at the Orange River; but when it had taken over the Diamond Fields, it began a northward march, which is now halting for a time on the southern frontier of Matabeleland. Its area is 275,000 square miles. Its government is democratic. The Crown appoints a Governor and High Commissioner; but the right of the Colony to govern itself through its own representatives is almost as absolute as that of any State in the American Union. There are two houses of Parliament, both elective; the Legislative Council consists of 23 members, the House of Assembly of 79. The franchise is not denied to the natives on the ground of colour; but the representatives are all white.

The population of Cape Colony in 1891 was 1,600,000, of whom only 380,000 were white. The Dutch dwell in the country, and preponderate in the Western province. The English flock to the towns and are strongest in the East. There are about 3,000 miles of railway built or building. The chief exports in 1896 to the United Kingdom were: Diamonds, £4,500,000; wool (sheep), £2,330,000; wool (goat), £490,000; ostrich feathers, £490,000; copper ore, £300,000. Altogether the total exports amounted to £17,000,000, while the imports were about £18,000,000.

The central feature of South Africa is its mountainous plateau. At about 150 miles from the seaboard the mountains rise in a lofty table-land, which stretches over 1,000 miles northward. It is on this table-land Europeans live and thrive.

The colony of Natal was first colonised in 1824 by a handful of Englishmen. The Boers tried to effect a lodgment in the country, but were beaten by the Zulus who occupied the land, and shortly after

the Governor of the Cape formally annexed Natal to the Cape. It lies fronting the Indian Ocean with a seaboard of
180 miles. Durban is the only port. It
has 420 miles of railway which, as is usual
in South Africa, are owned and worked
by the Government. The area is about
20,000 square miles, its population
540,000, of whom not 50,000 are white.
There are 40,000 Indian coolies, but the
enormous majority of the population are
Zulus. The country is mountainous, fertile, and healthy. It contains coal, and
yields tropical produce. Its exports in
1896 included wool, £600,000; coal,
£100,000. Its imports were £6,400,000,
but most of these were for the Transvaal.
The exports were only £2,000,000.

Between Natal and the Cape there are
the two native locations, or reserves, of
Basutoland and Pondoland. The latter was
annexed to the Cape quite recently. Basutoland is a native State of 250,000 population. The chiefs govern their own people, subject to the control of the British
Commission. Basutoland is 10,000 square

miles in extent, has a delightful climate, is well watered, very mountainous, and produces great quantities of cattle and of grain; revenue, £45,000; exports and imports, £300,000. To the north of Natal lies Zululand, chiefly famous for the war of 1879. It was not annexed until 1887, when part of the territory had been taken by the Boers. It is very largely kept as a native reserve, Europeans being only permitted to settle in one district. It is technically described as a British territory governed by a Resident Commissioner and chief magistrate under the Governor of Natal.

The two Republics of the Transvaal and of the Orange Free State lie between Natal and the northward extension of the Cape Colony. The Orange Free State is an inoffensive pastoral community of Boers. The Transvaal was a great ranch. It is now, thanks chiefly to the extraordinary gold reef on which Johannesburg stands, one of the greatest gold-producing countries in the world. It is an anomaly and an anachronism. Nowhere else in the whole world is an overwhelming majority of English-speaking men governed by a minority, speaking a foreign tongue, without any voice in the framing of their own laws and without any rights as citizens. It will pass, and the Transvaal will take its natural place in the federation of united South Africa.

On the west of the Transvaal stretches the vast expanse of the Protectorate of Bechuanaland, now traversed by the railway to Matabeleland, which is, however, but small compensation for the rinderpest which has swept off the herds of South Africa.

To the north lies the land of controversy and of mystery, the famous Charterland of Rhodesia, a territory many times larger than the German Empire, which has been reclaimed from savagery to colonisation and civilisation by the genius of the only millionaire with imagination which the century has brought forth. The British South African Company, which in 1889 received a Royal Charter authorising it to develop and administer

the lands lying between Bechuanaland
and the Zambezi, was the creation of Mr.
Rhodes's brain.   Mr. Rhodes, the Diamond King of South Africa, had a soul
above diamonds.   He saw that the
territory lying north of Bechuanaland
would be snapped up by the Germans or
secured for ranching by the Boers trek-
king from the Transvaal. He conceived
the idea of creating a joint stock company
with a capital of two millions and more
which would enable him "to paint the
African map British red" all the way
up to the Zambezi. The Imperial Government absolutely refused to expend a
pound on any such enterprise.   Mr.
Rhodes undertook to raise the money
and to direct the operation. The Government, believing, as they said, that
such a chartered company could "relieve
Her Majesty's Government from diplomatic difficulties and heavy expenditure,"
granted the charter.

Then Mr. Rhodes set to work. He put
his own money into the Company, and
others, inspired by a similar enthusiasm,

joined their capital to his. On June 28th, 1890, the pioneer expedition of 200 Europeans and 150 labourers, accompanied by 500 mounted police, set out to take possession of the Land of Ophir. They cut a road for 400 miles across the country, established posts and stations; and at last were disbanded at Fort Salisbury on September 19th, having established themselves in Mashonaland at a net cost of £89,285 10s. 0d. without firing a shot or spending a life. Settlers in search of gold poured into the country. To feed them, it was necessary to open a way to the sea at Beira, and this brought them into sharp collision with the Portuguese. The difficulty was arranged by a concession for the construction of a railway from the sea to the upland held by the Company, over which goods can be brought without paying any other tax but a transit duty of three per cent. The mines in Mashonaland were in full work when a new difficulty loomed on the western frontier of the new colony. Lobengula, the Chief of the warlike Matabele, was urged by his young warriors to allow them to flash their spears on the newcomers. He resisted for a time, but at last he gave way. An *impi* threatened the miners with destruction. Mr. Rhodes instantly took action. Placing £50,000 to the credit of the Company, he ordered Dr. Jameson to raise and equip an expeditionary force and to march on Buluwayo, Lobengula's kraal. One little force, 1,227 strong, of whom only 672 were whites, marched from the east; another of 445 of the Bechuanaland police came from the south. Against them Lobengula hurled first 5,000, then 7,000 of his best fighting men. They dashed themselves to pieces against the British *laager*. Buluwayo was captured, Lobengula fled, and Mr. Rhodes found himself in possession of Matabeleland. His force had only lost 84 men killed and 55 wounded. The total cost of the war was only £113,488 2s. 11d. This was in 1893. The success was too brilliant and too complete. It tempted Dr. Jameson to essay the daring raid on the Transvaal which in the early

days of 1895 led to so overwhelming a
disaster. Not only was Dr. Jameson's
force made prisoners, but the Matabele,
seeing the country denuded of its usual
garrison, rose in revolt. Then the Imperial authorities were compelled to inter-
vene, and send up troops to assist the
colonists to hold their own against the
insurgent natives. Mr. Rhodes, although
in disgrace, and stripped of all his offices,
was still the master of the situation. The
natives trusted him and accepted terms of
peace on his guaranty. After the suppression of the revolt the constitution of
the Charter was modified so as to place
the control of the armed forces of the Company in the hands of a representative of
the Crown.

The future of Rhodesia, which covers a
region of 750,000 square miles stretching from the Transvaal to Tanganyika,
depends upon the quantity of paying gold
that may be discovered. Plenty of aurif-
erous mineral exists, but until the stamps
needed to crush the ore can be brought
up, nothing can be said positively as to

the fate of the millions which have been
invested under the ægis of the Chartered
Company.   Mr. Rhodes himself is as confident as ever in the future of the country
that bears his name.   It will, he believes,
yield good dividends as well as good politics — but of the two he is much more
anxious about the latter.

History is still in the making in South
Africa; but unless all past experience
fails us as a guide to the probabilities of
the future, the hold on South Africa now
acquired by the English-speaking race will
never be relaxed.   The Cape is the key-
stone of the arch of the British Empire.
Without the coaling stations at Simon's
Bay, steam communication between Britain and Australia would be difficult, if not
impossible.   Hence the retention of the
Cape, and all that is necessary to the
safety of the Cape, is one of the few
things which, if threatened, the British at
home and over-sea regard as necessary to
fight for without discussion and without
phrase.

THE GERMAN EMPIRE IN AFRICA.

6

THE GERMAN EMPIRE IN AFRICA.

BY F. BLEY,

Late District Governor in East Africa, and Member of the German East African Society.

IT was the political principle of the German Government up to very recent times not to seek colonial aggrandisement. Prince Bismarck took possession of African lands mainly because of their possible worth, as objects of future barter. A colony had been founded in southern Brazil by a union of patriots in Hamburg as early as 1848; but this idea of obtaining a transmarine outlet for surplus German enterprise fell in abeyance with so many other popular ideals of that revolutionary year.

The nation lived to see the axiom set up that the flag of the Fatherland was to follow, not precede German merchantmen or pioneers, and to hear from the lips of the Imperial Chancellor, Count Caprivi, that " the worst thing that any one could do to Germany would be to give it the whole of Africa."

In contrast to this view stands the opinion of the men who are practically active in colonial affairs; they believe that the future of the German race will be determined essentially upon the soil of Africa. And, indeed, it is only necessary to glance at the map of the great Dark Continent, and contemplate the historic struggle of the Low German Boers against the aggressive tendencies of Great Britain, to find a support for this hypothesis.

The Germans received the accounts of Krapf, Mauch, Rohlf, and Schweinfurth, their native explorers in Africa, with sceptical indifference. On the other side of the canal the English greeted the discoveries of Burton, Speke, and even those of Stanley, as self-evident facts, saying to themselves, in accordance with their wonted material sense, that the interior of Africa could not be a sun-parched desert, possibly because mighty rivers flowed down from the interior, and products were brought away from it by traders.

If the English Government did not at once seize the territory thus recognised as fertile and valuable, the reason lay in the fact of its having its hands full at the time in other parts of the world, as well as in the fact that it remained in ignorance of the change which had taken place in the German character under the guidance of Prince Bismarck. From a people given up to romantic idealism, a nation of ironlike hardness of will had been evolved, which, when the partition of Africa began, was to demand its due share of spoils and conquests.

England looked on while Germany acquired African territory in the east and west with surprise and good-natured mockery at first. But when it saw that the land-rat had not fallen into the water by accident, but knew how to swim, and intended to keep on, British envy was aroused; and by degrees it has learned to see in Germany a power which it is destined to encounter henceforth, not only

in the Dark Continent, but in every other
part of the world.

In the beginning, this jealousy was
exerted with some success. From longi-
tude 48° east, around Cape Guardafui to
Rovuma, Dr. Peters had laid claim to the
coast-lands in the name of Germany. And
if German diplomacy had acquiesced in
his plans, the flag of Germany would be
waving to-day over Uganda and the pal-
aces of the Sultan of Zanzibar. Instead
of this the Government signed one treaty
after another, allowing that which had
been acquired *de facto* to become a subject of dispute and the claims of others,
while the German people, in the ingrati-
tude it showed to the founder of its East
African colonies, proved once again its
want of insight into the historic task of
helping to extend civilisation.

Fortunately, that part of East Africa
which was assured to Germany is the
more valuable one. Its boundaries in-
close an area of 885,000 square kilometres,
which is to say an area twice as large as
the German Empire. In this territory lie

Lake Tanganyika, Lake Victoria, and the
north side of the Nyassa. The wonderful
summit of the ice-covered Kilimanjaro
sends from its fountain sources the clear,
sparkling rivers of the Pangani, while the
rivers Wami, Lungerengere, and Kingani
have their origin in the wooded sides of
Usagara and Ukami, which remind one
of the mountainous region of the Hartz
and the Salz Kammergut.

The Rufiji River is navigable for boats
of $2\frac{1}{2}$ metres displacement as far as the
Pangani Cataracts, and the seaboard of
this province is the richest in harbours of
all the East African coast.

The natives, who belong essentially to
the Bantu race, are divided into several
branches with various traits. On the
whole they are tractable, and may be
trained to work if they are treated with
justice and humanity. Nor is a certain
superior intelligence and capacity for reflection wanting to them. It happened
more than once during my sojourn among
them that their chieftains expressed a
sense of their own native want of the

talent for organisation. "It is good you are here, lord," the chieftain in my station, Usungula, declared often. "You understand things better than we do. Look at this house. It is made of the clay of our earth, and with the hands of our bodies; but it was your head that gave to it regularity and great size. You take the axe to labour, and the hatred of brothers you allay by treaties of peace. You alone are lord, and it is well. Each of us strove to be master, and none was. But you are rich; you have pieces of shining silver, and the caravans bring you more continually for our people. We went in rags, and hunger ate at our vitals in the wet seasons of the year. We have clothes now in our huts as fine as those of Arabic traders, and we possess bright rupees with which to buy us goats and fowls and rice when we are hungry. You are lord, for you knew how to order all things so as to make them flow even and smooth as the little rains."

In regard to its soil, East Africa affords considerable variety, as is evident, indeed, that it must, by reason of its topography. There are no mighty primeval forests, such as cover the mountain districts of Ceylon and Sumatra; but the wooded mountain districts of Usambara, Usagara, Ukami, and Ukonde, as well as its boundary districts of Kilimanjaro, are well suited for plantations to be carried on after the manner of those of the Dutch; while in the bottom-lands, sugar-cane, tobacco, rice, and certain kinds of spices flourish luxuriantly.

The capital of the province of Dar-es-Salaam, in the point of construction, is a pattern city, and, what is the chief thing, the plantations of Usambara are making brilliant progress. The coffee raised there is rapidly winning a market for itself. In short, there can exist no doubt but that German East Africa will succeed before long in furnishing valuable agricultural products in exchange for the productions of German industry. Our capitalists perceive this, too, for they are investing more and more in East African stocks.

Many of the original African products

are doomed to fall way, and ultimately to entirely disappear. Copal will probably begin to be furnished from the far interior after the supply has been exhausted on the coast-land, and continue to be an article of trade for some years to come, copal-trees being found inland, indicating the existence of this fossil gum there. But the days of the ivory trade are numbered; it must end with the vanishing of the elephant herds. This, to my mind, is a consummation devoutly to be wished, for with the passing away of these herds will cease the brutal hunting of the natives as slaves to carry tusks; and, possibly, the few remaining animals may then be trained for beasts of burden, as elephants are in India. With no more slave raids, there will likewise end the internecine wars which have hindered the natural increase of the native population hitherto. In the long run, the negro comprises the chief wealth of Africa. The advance of civilisation and its need for increasing quantities of manufactured goods depends upon the multiplication of population.

East Africa has an advantage over all tropical provinces belonging to Germany, in possessing, in the high lying district of Uhehe and the border mountains of the Nyassa, moist meadow-lands in which the usual unhealthy conditions of equatorial latitude are neutralised by an Alpine-like climate.

The present Governor intends, with the aid of influential corporations, to make use of this most favoured locality by establishing a peasant settlement therein, in which case, I hope the settlement will devote its energies, not to raising grain, but to breeding cattle, raising ostrich herds, and the like, after the manner followed by the Boers in the Orange Free State. The climate and soil of the Nyassa district and Uhehe resemble those of the Free State in all particulars. What will be the result of the transplanting of a colony of white men to these mountain regions is an open question. Everything appears favourable to the increase of the Caucasian race there.

The prospects for the future in the two other chief possessions of West Africa are

similar to those of German East Africa,
except, indeed, as to what concerns the
two last mentioned districts. In Togo
and Kamerun, the hinterland had been
allowed to be deplorably cut into, and
partly cut off, by other Powers. It was
above all in the Togo treaties that the
German Government erred gravely, inasmuch as, for the specious gain of a
strip of coast twenty-five kilometres long,
it relinquished the piece of territory which
connected its possessions with the Niger
River. Borgu and Gurma were ceded to
France, and with the concession the expansion of German influence was relinquished toward the north. The land
which remains in our possession, however,
is most valuable. It is traversed by a
double range of mountains, which rise
abruptly from an undulating plain, and
give origin to numerous rivers which flow
from their sides to the coast, — the Mono,
Haho, Sio, Tojie, and the tributaries of
the Volta: Kalagba, Djavoe, Deine,
Konsu, Asukoho, and Oti. The great
Volta itself flows through the highland

in a broad valley, and is navigable from
Kratji on downward.

Togo could be reckoned among the
countries of the Southern Hemisphere as
far as the climate is concerned, for the
season of maximum heat corresponds with
the Northern winter, and that of minimum heat to the Northern summer. The
coldest months are those of July and
August. The principal products of the
soil are brought to the trading factories
that have been established in the province
by native negroes, who compose a branch
of the Sûdan negroes, and possess the
same energetic traits which distinguish
the Sûdanese.

Among these products are palm-tree-oil
and nuts, copra, cocoanuts, gutta-percha,
and ivory. Plantations also of coffee and
Manihot Glaziovii have been laid out.

Still more favourable than Togo seems
to be the situation of the plantations in
Kamerun; for the mountains of the province draw near the coast, and their western slope affords, in its soil of decayed
lava, with plentiful rainfalls, the most ex-

cellent conditions for the cultivation of cocoa and coffee trees. Over half a million of cocoa-trees already stand on this slope, and new plantations are about to be started.

The other products are the same as in Togo. In the south a kind of coffee bush has been discovered, which may, perhaps, obtain importance some day as a staple article.

German Southwest Africa presents quite different conditions, being of a sub-tropical character, and suitable for European immigrants. It is the last territory acquired by Germany. Herr von Lüderitz bought it in the year 1883, without knowing much about it, and placed it under the protection of the Imperial flagship " Leipsic " in 1884.

It appeared to be of little worth. The coast, which stretches from Cunene to the Orange River, that is to say from a Portuguese to an English colony, is not merely inhospitable, it is dreadful. Sand-dunes squat like bands of crouching Titans on it and shift from place to place, burying all beneath them. The only harbour, Angra Pequeña, affords but a bad connection with the interior, and Walfisch Bay with its tolerable inlet into Damaraland, was in the hands of the all-grasping English. So the acquisition of Southwest Africa appeared a poor enough bargain, and Germans generally took it for granted that the wandering sand-hills could not so much as supply a turtle with water and food to keep it alive. But Lüderitz bethought himself of the fact that a flourishing export trade in ivory, ostrich feathers, gums, skins, and horns had been carried on from this country as late as 1860; and, granting that the game in the meanwhile might have become exterminated, still the grass-lands must remain which had supported it. Besides, as late as the development of Kimberley, in 1872, large numbers of cattle had been shipped from here to the country of the Boers. Hence fertile lands must lie somewhere, and Lüderitz thought he recognised them in the highlands of the interior.

Unfortunately, he met with his death on

an exploring tour, and before he had had
the time to convey his own growing conviction of the immense worth of Southwest Africa to his countrymen at home.
The Government was so ignorant that it
felt embarrassed and annoyed over the
need of settling with the heirs of the cour-
ageous man, and regarded the offer of a
syndicate in 1885 to purchase the Lüderitz family claims as a favour to the State.
Its inadequate protection, furthermore, and
its ill management of the province, encouraged the English to stir up the natives
to rebellion ; and these political difficulties
discouraged, of course, money investment.
Southwest Africa, in short, was considered
for a long time as a very bad job; and
Count Caprivi appears to have been prepared to cede it to England in 1890,
whenever an opportunity should occur.
It was public opinion chiefly which saved
the province to the German Crown; for
the scientific reports of travellers slowly
and surely aroused the people to a sense
of its potentialities, as well as the determi-
nation to hold for themselves what they

had acquired. The Government, in the mean time, however, had unfortunately granted two charters to English companies, — one to what is known as the Southwest African Company, in 1893, and a second to what became the South African Territories Land Company, in 1895 ; and these had to remain in force henceforth to the disadvantage of German interests. At the present time, the province can boast of an energetic and circumspect Governor. Major Leutwein not only facilitates immigration, but proposes to domesticate it by obtaining subsidies for the importation of such German women as are suitable to become the wives of German pioneers.

These settlements are not to be thought of as small farms, with careful tillage of the soil, like the farms of Iowa and Wisconsin, for example, but as resembling rather the ranch farms of Texas. Gardens and orchards, of course, will be cultivated in the vicinity of the trading and military posts, for the better welfare of the inhabitants ; and there are prospects of some of the more

fertile sites along the valley slopes being
turned into vineyards and tobacco plantations. But the main occupation of the
settlers must be cattle breeding for long
years to come.

Southwest Africa has a paradisiacal climate; nothing can surpass it. Although
the land lies two-thirds in the Tropic Zone,
and only one-third in the Temperate
Zone, the local configuration is such that
the temperature is everywhere moderate,
except in the district of Cunene and a few
inland sections. The air of the broad,
upland plains is pure and dry, and the
juicy verdure is encouraged into luxuriant
growth by the brilliance of the southern
sun. Alternating with the heat of the
day is a coolness of the night which benefits both man and beast alike. Hoar-frost
is no infrequent occurrence, and heavy
dews form during all the dry season. The
rainy season falls in December and January, and brings showers that fill the beds
of the rivers full to their brims. In summer the lower streams dry up, but the
water courses under the sand at no great

depth, and breaks out wherever there is a
rift, making puddles and small ponds.
Irrigation is an easy task, and, whenever
it shall be applied on a large scale, will
transform vast tracts of waste land into
pasture grounds.

As to that one great drawback of the
country, the so-called rinderpest, it is already being overcome. Applied science
is sure to put an end to the plague and
further infection from it.

Less likelihood exists of the province
getting rid of the moral hindrances which
the bureaucratic disposition of the Government is laying constantly in the way of
its free development. I reckon among
these the systematic attempt which is kept
up to exclude Boers from the country.
Is it from an apprehension of their spread-
ing a spirit of Republican independence
therein? The Boers are, indeed, intract-
able in their half-civilised devotion to the
idea of political liberty; but, at the same
time, they compose the best conceivable
material for what may be termed a colonising plant. They are industrious, tem-

perate, tough in body, and, above all, experienced particularly in just those things which pertain to South African farming and cattle raising. It is the very element which is needed by Germany to aid in settling its new African lands.

The present deprivation which the Government's action lays upon the colony, however, is not the only one; still more to be regretted is likely to be the future consequences that must flow from neglect of Boer good will and welfare. The struggle between the Dutch and English in South Africa would be accelerated to an end, if a power like Germany afforded open aid to the Dutch. At present the Boers wish to become neither German nor English; but they will be unable to resist subjection in the long run of time; and as natural affinity will draw them ultimately to the lap of Germany, the better will it be for the Germans, the more widespread and prosperous they have become. The Government ought to leave no stone unturned to encourage its subjects to try to understand and appreciate the peculiar

ways and opinions of the Boers. The
future of the white race in Africa depends
upon the rapidity with which a mutual
understanding between the two Teutonic
branches of it can be developed.

The German Government may be
brought to perceive this, and to let minor
political considerations drop into abeyance, in order to adjust its policy in accordance with the one great question at
stake. But at present its task appears to
be to seek colonial aggrandisement *per se ;*
it is even emulating Great Britain in encouraging colonial commerce, all of which
is a great step in advance beyond its
former indifference to matters colonial.
The final comprehensive grasp of the subject of African colonisation, however, from
the point of view of the political future
is still wanting. At least no evidences
of such grasp of the subject are visible
as yet to men working in Africa.

In conclusion, a word may be added in
respect to railways in the German African
provinces. In East Africa a road extends
from Tanga to Korogwe, and will be carried

to the Kilimanjaro. Two other roads are planned, one from Dar-es-Salaam through Usaramo, Ukami, Usagara to the Victoria Nyanza, another from Rufiji to the Pangani Falls.

In Southwest Africa there is a railway from Swakopmund to Windhoek.

THE FRENCH EMPIRE
IN AFRICA.

THE FRENCH EMPIRE IN AFRICA.

BY M. PAUL GUIEYSSE,

Deputy and Ex-Minister of the Colonies.

TWENTY years ago Stanley descended the Kongo, and thus opened its immense basin to European cupidity. The carving up of the Black Continent has nearly been completed, though its consequences may still give rise to many discussions. But the sphere of action of each of the invading nations is now clearly traced, and the difficulties that spring up from time to time are due to a narrow sentiment and a misunderstanding of true economic interests, which lead to an attempt to substitute artificial limits for rational and natural ones.

The present century has witnessed the geographical conquest of Africa. To speak only of the northern regions, which are naturally subject to French influence, it may be recalled that a Frenchman, Caillé, was the first to penetrate, in 1828, into mysterious Timbuktu. At the same moment Clapperton, the Scotchman, discovered Lake Tchad and Sokoto, while Bath, in 1850, and Nachtigal, in 1869, explored the regions of the middle Niger to Lake Tchad, and thence to the Nile. Lenz reached Timbuktu in 1880, and Flatters, following out the plans of Duveyrier, fell before the attacks of the Tuaregs, while striving to connect Algeria with the Sûdan. The grand divisions of North Africa were settled. The French expeditions into the basin of the Upper Niger were about to begin and to continue without interruption down to the present day by the joining of the Sûdan with Dahomey, while a mission, under the command of Captain Marchand, connected the French posts on the Kongo and the Ubangi with the Nile.

France is one of the earliest nations established on the western coast of Africa. The Dieppe factories there rival those of Portugal as regards age. As early as

1626, the Senegal region attracted the traders of Normandy, one of whose companies bought the islet, situated at the mouth of the Senegal River, which became St. Louis. Under Louis XIV. the Royal Company took possession of the whole coast, stretching from the Bay of Arguin to Gorée, and these territories were declared to belong to France by the Treaty of Nimeguen. Trade in gums, hides, and ivory brought good returns. But the European traders were stationed only along the coasts; as was the case in fact, till recent years, all the way to Gabûn. A few small fortified store-houses sufficed to protect the traders against the treachery of the native chiefs.

In 1697 the Governor of Senegal, André Brue, went up the river, entered into negotiations with the chiefs along the banks, and concluded with them treaties of commerce and friendship. But the wars in Europe caused the colony to fall into the hands of the English, who lost it, retook it, but, finally, ceded it to France in the general peace of 1815. It was not till

1854 that the enterprise began by André
Brue could be taken up seriously by
the real creator of Senegal, General
Faidherbe.

The inhabitants of the region belonged
to various races. On the right bank were
the Trarza Moors, an almost white race,
mingled with half-breeds and blacks, one
of the results of slavery. Successive treaties had succeeded in getting them to
abandon the few settlements which they
had on the left bank. An agricultural
and pastoral people, their interests com-
manded them to live in peace with us.
On the left bank and in the upper valley
were pressed together the Puls or Fulahs,
of a dark red hue, who came from the
East and who were shepherds and merchants ; the Toucouleurs, half-breeds,
farmers for the most part ; and many
negroes, pushed back by the Puls, and
with no definite past history, but under
Mohammedan influence, either through
force or simply through contact, and, like
the Toucouleurs, given up to fetichism.
The Woloffs were in majority in these

negro races. They are the most intelligent and are very good labourers, so that there is every reason for us to cultivate their good will.

The most profound peace now reigns through this region, with no danger of its being broken, and, consequently, prosperity is increasing daily. The railroad from St. Louis to Dakar passes through fertile fields where scarcely two years ago military acts of repression were necessary. But when Faidherbe wished to proceed to the occupation of Upper Senegal, he had first to break the power at Medina, of the Toucouleur Marabout, El Hadji Homar, whose empire extended from Lake Tchad to Senegal, and who, by terrorising and fanaticising the inhabitants, hoped to be able to push us back into the sea.

Since then the advance of French influence in those regions has been more or less rapid, but always continuous. The negro empires rise up in a night, and melt away quite as quickly. Based on the momentary power and ascendency of a Marabout, they disappear with him. The grand influence of Timbuktu, which was once exerted over the whole upper and middle region of the Niger basin, had a solid reason for its existence; for the geographical position of the city made it the commercial centre of all the surrounding regions, and causes it to survive its political renown which exists no longer. The Empire of Ahmadon, son of El Hadji Homar, was no exception to the general rule.

The expeditions of Borgnis-Desbordes, Gallieni, and Archinard pushed back, but not without considerable difficulty because of the feeble means at their disposal, the bands of pillagers and devastators occupying the right bank of the Niger. The last of these chiefs, who exists only by terrorising and massacring the inoffensive inhabitants, is Samory, who has recently won such an unenviable reputation by betraying and assassinating an officer sent to confer with him. He is now carrying on his operations on the confines of Sierra Leone, Liberia, and the Ivory Coast, being driven more and more into a corner. An end must be put to this bandit, who yearly sacrifices a hundred thousand unfortunate beings in order that he may preserve his power.

The Niger, once in our possession, and joined by a chain of forts and soon by a railroad to Senegal, the rather inaccessible region of Futa-Jallon, which was already under our protectorate, ought to become an annex of our possessions. This is now the case. Senegal is connected directly with our colony on the Ivory Coast. The settling of the boundaries with the little English and Portuguese colonies of Gambia, which are little else than indentures into our territories, and especially with Sierra Leone and Liberia, has now been brought about by definite treaties, so that France is at last free to advance into the Upper Niger region by way of Senegal, or by the new route in process of construction, which starts at Konakry, on the coast, and passes along the Futa-Jallon country.

The Upper Niger, which resembles the Nile in its periodic and fertilising overflows, waters a wonderfully rich region inhabited by peaceable dwellers who ask only to live in quiet and security, and who could promptly repair the evils caused by the devastators from whom we have delivered them. This region, which is within our reach, has a great future before it. This is proved by the whole history of Timbuktu, of which we have lately come into possession without any resistance; in fact, with the complicity of its inhabitants, whom we have thus delivered from the tyranny of the Tuaregs.

Timbuktu is on the confines of the desert, and the great commercial centre for all the products brought there by the camel caravans and other means of transport of the neighbouring or distant tribes. Though its trade has considerably fallen off, it is rapidly picking up again, — a trade which, at the beginning of the present century was still valued at more than twenty million dollars annually. The security which it will now enjoy under France will soon restore to the town its old importance.

The chief scourge of the Sahara and at the same time the conductors of the Timbuktu caravans are the Tuaregs, who are beginning to feel their dependence on us since our discovery of the grand reservoir lakes which play for the Niger the same part—in fact, a still more important one—that the ancient Lake Mœris did for the Nile. The important town of Bassikunu, which these lakes separate from Timbuktu, has just been taken possession of, and the vast region of which it is the capital has become our territory. This whole country is destined to enjoy a wonderful future, provided peace can be preserved, so that it becomes the interest and duty of France to protect the inhabitants against all incursions which, in fact, are becoming more and more rare.

The Niger region has become an object of cupidity to all the nations which had, but a short time ago, simple trading posts along the coast of the Gulf of Guinea. The destruction of the bloody despots of Dahomey and Ashanti, by France and England, has been an inestimable benefit to all the peaceable peoples of the interior. But France occupies a preponderant position in these regions. By means of her Ivory Coast Colony her possessions extend to the Kongo States, traversed a few years ago for the first time by Binger, and which are the centre of the campaign against Samory. Our frontier line on the west, in the direction of Liberia and Sierra Leone, has been fixed by treaties, and on the east, where lie the English Gold Coast Colony and the German Togo, a few concessions have brought about a similar result; so that we are now in complete possession of all the territory lying between these colonies and the course of the Niger. The actual occupation of these lands was brought about only a few months ago. Scarcely had Lieutenant Hourst of our navy accomplished the whole descent of the Niger, than the expeditions which had started simultaneously from the Sûdan and Dahomey, under Lieutenant Voulet and Captain Baud, effected a junction, after having established posts in all the principal centres of the Niger region. But one point remains unsettled,—fixing the northern boundary of French Dahomey between that colony and the English Lagos. This is in fact "the Niger question," which is now occupying the attention of the French and English Foreign Offices.

While Stanley was finishing the general exploration of the Kongo, and the King of the Belgians was bringing about the formation of the Independent Kongo State, Brazza, going up the course of the Ogove, reached by the Alima, an affluent of the Kongo, Stanley Pool, where he founded Brazzaville. This was the origin of the French Kongo State, which is in communication with Lake Tchad by the navigable river Shari and with the Nile by the Bahr-el-Ghazal.

The important results which the future has in store for this part of Africa, and the grave differences arising on every side, caused the bringing together of the Berlin Congress, which regulated these various difficulties. One of the principal

of these decisions was the proclamation
of the free navigation of the Kongo and
Niger Rivers, and a declaration that a
tax must be levied on all nations alike
which used these rivers, these moneys to
be employed for the general expenses of
administration, etc. France gave her full
consent to this regulation, and it is the
realisation of this stipulation that she
firmly demands to-day in the case of the
Niger.

The course of the Niger is interrupted
at Bussa, north of Dahomey, by rapids
which render navigation very difficult.
Furthermore, the claims — I may almost
say, the reprehensible acts — of the Royal
Niger Company have rendered access to
the river almost impossible for Europeans.
France has unfortunately shown, in the
treatment of this affair, a feebleness or a
negligence which is greatly to be regretted, and which does but little credit
to our diplomacy. The abandonment of
the Mizon Mission at Yola, on the Upper
Binue, south of Lake Tchad, and of the
Aremberg post created by Toutée, on

the right bank of the Niger below Bussa,
were acts of culpable condescension to
England.

During the past year these faults have
been partly repaired by the arrival at
Bussa of Lieutenant Bretonnet, of the
French Navy, who has been received in
a friendly manner by the Chief of that
region. It is absolutely indispensable
that we hold this town in order that the
French Niger region may have a practicable communication with the sea. At
this moment a commission is settling the
question of the boundary line between
Dahomey and Lagos. France cannot
abandon the results obtained by Decœur,
Toutée, Bellot, and so many other of her
noble sons. France and England will
not fall out over details; but we occupy
those regions legally, by treaties with the
native chiefs and, effectively, by the planting there of our standard. It will be
dangerous for the English to disturb us.
We have yielded too often to English
pretensions. When we decide to speak
to England in a firm tone, especially when

we have justice on our side, she will have to give way.[1]

To sum up the situation in the Niger region, it may be said that this magnificent result may now be considered accomplished ; the whole vast territory is French up to the recognised limits of the foreign colonies. There is but one shadow in the picture, Samory, who cannot, however, hold out much longer. He once disposed of, prosperity will then reign, without serious danger of any interruption, throughout these five districts, which ask only to be left to live in peace under our protectorate, and whose intelligent inhabitants appreciate with feelings of real joy our gentle influence.

Quite other are the peoples over whom France rules in her Kongo State. There begin the regions which, along with those of Guinea, were so long the inexhaustible source whence were drawn the slaves for the Antilles and America ; and the reports of Speke, Burton, Livingstone, and others have shown at the price of what

1 See note on p. 32.

monstrous cruelties and massacres the
trading Arabs, who exploited the eastern
part, obtained the slaves necessary for the
transporting of ivory and other merchandise. It was none too soon for the Belgians and French, who occupy the whole
basin of the Kongo, to put an end to this
horrible state of things. The way of pro-
ceeding of the two nations is quite different, for while we hear too often of conflicts
and revolts in the Free State, it may be
permitted to point out that France has
only a few hundred Senegalian soldiers
on the Kongo and its chief affluent, the
Ubangi.

The first tribes one meets in these
Kongo regions on leaving the coast are
genuine savages, always at war with one
another, often cannibals, but who can be
easily managed if strict rules of justice
and equity are observed. The men are
good only as carriers and paddlers, and
are as yet incapable of performing regular
labour. But this can be changed by a
slow and continual effort on our part.
The farther you recede from the coast,

greater and greater becomes the primitive barbarity. But when, by the Shari River, which empties into Lake Tchad, and along whose waters float our steam-launches, or by the Ubangi, you approach the districts under Mussulman influence, the situation improves.

In passing around Lake Tchad, whose western and southern shores are partly within the zone of the influence of the English of the Niger and of the Germans of Kamerun, the French possessions are found to be brought into contact with the Sûdanese or rather Saharian regions, great stretches of territory which are often but deserts, and whose rare inhabitants, the Tuaregs, still inspire great fear. By the Ubangi River one reaches the States of the Sultans Rafaï and Zemio, with whom we are on friendly terms on account of our common interests. In giving them our support, we enable them to exert an influence over those confused masses who participate in the Mahdist movement and to resist them. It was through the aid of Zemio that Marchand was able to reach the basin of the Bahr-el-Ghazal, to descend one of its water-courses, and at this moment, doubtless, gunboats, flying the French flag, float on the Nile at Fashoda. Abyssinia is not far away. It must not be forgotten that the Harrar Railroad, whose construction is begun, and whose prolongation toward the interior is simply a matter of time, starts from our possessions of Djibouti, on the Gulf of Tadjurah, at the entrance to the Red Sea. It is unnecessary to dwell on the consequences to Egypt and the Egyptian provinces of the Upper Nile which will spring from this road.

Nothing need be said of Algeria and Tunis, as they are under a regular admin-istration, and, in this respect, may almost be classed among European nations. It must be admitted, however, that there always exists the danger in those regions of a revolt, due to Mussulman fanaticism, which has grown all the more arrogant as a result of the shameful feebleness of what is called oddly enough "the Concert of Europe." Tottering Morocco, which is kept standing only because of the rivalries between the Powers, may play at any moment an important part in a general uprising, which would spread as far as Tripoli. But the farther France penetrates into the Sahara, occupying new oases and making fresh treaties with the Tuaregs, who are so hard to win over, but who can be depended upon having once given their word, the greater is the probability of obtaining in these northern parts of Africa a state of stability and security. When one has to do with religious fanaticism, force alone must be counted upon. By showing that a revolt will be repressed without pity, a check may be put to a movement for the starting of one.

As regards the great island of Madagascar, it stands so without Africa proper that I simply mention it here in passing. It is a world apart.

Will the French know how to make the most of the vast domain which is now open to them in the Black Continent? The changes at present going on in the

French public mind are happily very significant. Colonial expansion in this country was checked by the wars of the Revolution and the Empire. But a movement in that direction has now most decidedly set in again. Just as under the ancient régime the younger sons of noble families sought their fortune in foreign parts, so now the children of the bourgeoisie, not being able to find occupations at home, are beginning to turn their faces toward the colonies. May my fellow-countrymen recover that old spirit of initiative, and renew that early taste for colonisation which produced such brilliant results, always bearing in mind that it was not Frenchmen who lost their colonies, but the miserable governments which they too long permitted to exist.

THE INDEPENDENT KONGO STATE.

THE INDEPENDENT KONGO STATE.

BY LIEUT. CHARLES LEMAIRE,

Ex-Commissioner of the Equator District of the Kongo State.

THE astonishing creation of a vast free State, which has, in twenty years, completely changed the greatest river basin of the world, till then profoundly buried in darkness and barbarism, and made it a land of order and civilisation, — this astounding transformation is due to the will of a single man. Before mounting the Belgian throne, the then Duke de Brabant, in a volume entitled "The Complement of the Work of 1830," pointed out in the most elevated language the necessity for Belgians to have a colony beyond the seas. Become King, this same prince, Leopold II, now sovereign of the Independent Kongo State, turned his attention forthwith toward carrying out this dream of many years.

In 1876 the King brought together in his palace the Brussels Geographical Congress, composed of well-known men of learning, geographers, and explorers of all nations. This was the origin of the International African Society, whose aim was to create an uninterrupted chain of stations from the eastern coast to the great lakes discovered by Livingstone. This meant the penetrating into equatorial Africa from the east, as all attempts from the west had failed.

The best known of these expeditions from the west was that placed by the English Admiralty under the orders of Capt. James K. Tuckey. In 1816 Tuckey went up the Kongo to a distance of some 170 miles, but lost eighteen men in four months, which seemed to check further attempts in that direction.

On August 9th, 1877, a man arrived at the mouth of the Kongo and said : " It is now 999 days since I left Zanzibar. I have seen all the lands known to the Arabs of the East, and during 281 days I have traversed countries which no white man ever saw before. I have sailed along over 1,500 miles of a wonderful river, and, by making a détour of some 150 miles, I have been able to pass around forty cataracts."

The man who told this wonderful tale was Stanley, who had thus completed the discoveries of Livingstone, and who, in order to solve the problem of the Kongo, which could not be approached from the west, had taken it at the other end and had descended from Nyangwe to Banana, telling of his thirty-two fights which he had had with cannibals along the unknown river, of the seven equatorial cataracts (to-day Stanley Falls), of the thirty-two falls, of terrible privations, deaths, massacres, etc.

For the third time Africa had now been crossed from the Orient to the Occident. After Livingstone and Cameron, Stanley had traversed those regions marked on the maps as *terra incognita*. Doubtless an enthusiastic welcome awaited the brave adventurer. Not at all. Europe pretended to see in Stanley signs of an impostor, and mistrusted him. But he inspired confidence in the King of the Belgians, and from this confidence was to spring the future State of Kongo.

In 1873, at the suggestion and under the auspices of Leopold II, the Committee for the Study of the Upper Kongo was formed. Its purpose was to do on the West Coast what the International African Society was endeavouring to accomplish on the East Coast. This new organisation also determined to foster commercial development, which is the best way to get into contact with the negroes.

An expedition, whose aim was the study of this whole question in detail and on the spot, was immediately organised and placed under the orders of Stanley, who, in 1879, again appeared at the mouth of the Kongo, and set to work to perform the duties assigned him. These duties were to examine into the navigability of the river and its affluents, to enter into peaceful commercial and political relations with the natives, to secure territorial concessions, to establish posts, conclude treaties, to learn what were the exploitable riches of the region, to decide what lines of artificial communication could be opened, and particularly to find out if it would be possible to link, by means of a railroad, the Atlantic Coast with the river system of Central Africa. This programme reveals the long-cherished dream of Leopold II,—the desire to create an outlet for the industrial activity of his people, to spread the benefits of civilisation by means of commerce and labour, and to found, without the effusion of blood which characterised earlier conquests in Africa, a grand, rich colony that, later, could be handed over to Belgium.

Full of enthusiasm, Belgian officers begged to join the expedition, and, accompanied by them, Stanley sailed up the noble river and its branches, making treaties and dropping along its banks his agents, whom he inflamed with his own enterprising ardour. And in the footsteps of these bold pioneers followed missionaries, scientists, merchants, and,

curiously enough, even tourists, some of
whom were so filled with enthusiasm for
the enterprise that they asked to be allowed to share its dangers and hardships
alongside of the Belgians. Such, for instance, was Lieutenant Mohun, U. S. A.,
consular agent, charged by his Government with a mission to the Kongo, who
made this whole campaign.

In the end the decisive results obtained
by this Stanley expedition led the Committee for the Study of the Upper Kongo
to transform itself into an International
Kongo Association, so that the newly
explored territories could be brought
under a strong and independent administration, emanating from a duly established
authority, recognised as such by the principal nations of the world.

Toward the end of 1883, the International Kongo Association had in its
possession more than 10,000 treaties
signed by the native chiefs, who volun-
tarily ceded their sovereign rights over
the lands which they occupied. While
continuing its active work in Africa, the

Association entered into diplomatic relations with the Great Powers, in order to obtain from them the recognition of its sovereignty in the Kongo basin, and the enjoyment of the immunities and prerogatives of a State. The United States was first, on April 10th, 1884, to recognise the new State, and, seven months later, the German Empire followed this good example.

On November 15th, 1884, opened the Conference of Berlin, assembled to regulate, in a spirit of mutual amity, " the conditions which should assure the development of commerce on the Kongo and prevent contentions and misunderstandings." This memorable conference traced the limits of the conventional basin of the Kongo, indicated what the economic legislation should be for its government, declared its neutrality, that it should be under the protection of nations, that free navigation and liberty of conscience should be assured, that the slave-trade should be prohibited, and finally decided that, " in order to protect the native popu-

lation from the evils of war, all serious
differences concerning the limits, or within
the limits, of the territories designated by
the conference should be submitted to the
mediation of one or several Governments."

During the sittings of the Conference,
most European nations, imitating the example set by the United States and Germany, recognised the sovereignty of the
International Kongo Association, and the
Association itself having, on February
26th, 1885, adhered to the resolutions
promulgated by the Conference, Prince
Bismarck closed the assembly with a
speech in which he expressed best wishes
for the prosperity of the new State.

But a ruler for the State was necessary.
The Berlin Conference had unanimously
proposed Leopold II.   Thereupon the
Belgian Parliament authorised the King
to accept the new sovereignty by declar-
ing that " the union between Belgium and
the new State will be an exclusively personal one."   The Government was then
immediately organised, and in July, 1885,
the constitution of the Kongo State was

proclaimed at Banana and at all the stations of the interior districts.   In August
of the same year Leopold notified all the
Powers of the creation of the Independent
Kongo State and that he had become its
ruler.   The declaration of neutrality immediately followed, and the State was
thus definitely founded.

By this time Stanley had, by the aid
of three little steamers, got up the river
as high as Stanley Falls, and had explored
several of its affluents, while still others
were explored by his successors, so that
there could be no longer any doubt as to
what there was in that great white blank
found on even the latest maps at that
time.   It had been learned that at some
200 miles from Matadi, which the great
ocean steamers could reach, spread out
an incomparable river system, some 20,000
miles of whose banks, accessible to steamers, had been visited.   The world now
knows that this immense basin was a
hundred times larger than Belgium, that
it was once a vast fresh-water lake, which
buried for a time the fecundity of the

submerged soil; that this great plain was virgin, waiting for a comer; that it was covered with the richest of tropical vegetation, and was cut up by a network of navigable waters, the like of which could be found, probably, nowhere else on the globe,— for there is no point on it more than sixty miles from a river-bank; that the region was peopled with millions of negroes, those incomparable labourers of the tropics.

But Stanley declared to all who would listen that the full possibilities of the region could be realised only through the instrumentality of a railway which should connect Matadi with Leopoldville. He further stated that no other road was necessary unless one wished to reach the most distant confines of Central Africa and to pass from the basin of the Kongo into that of the Tchad, the Nile, and the Zambezi. Thereupon came to the aid of the King daring men who promised to build the road from the ocean to Stanley Pool. Nothing daunted them,— neither numerous deaths, the continual disap-

pointments at the start, nor the unmerited
attacks of low politicians. So from 1889,
the year when the work began in Matadi,
until the present moment, the gigantic
labour has gone on, so slowly at first that
even the most sanguine lost heart, then
faster and faster, till finally the whistle
of the first locomotive from Matadi reached
Stanley Pool and was answered by the
whistles of the steamers on the Upper
Kongo. This memorable event happened
at the moment I was writing these lines;
and I can easily imagine the emotion it
must have occasioned in the hearts of
the white men assembled on that occasion
from every part of the Pool.

Under the pressure of political parties,
the Belgian Government, which had ac-
corded to the Kongo Railway undertaking a certain amount of pecuniary support,
was forced to send out in 1895 a technical
commission charged with drawing up a
report on the condition of the work already finished or under way, on the possi-
bility of completing the whole enterprise,
and on the amount of traffic which would

probably occur on the line. This commission, which was extremely cautious in its statements, reported that the work on the road was well done, that the rolling stock was well made and properly mounted, that the trains ran regularly, that the whole labour could be finished by the end of 1900, and that the road could do an annual business amounting to 30,000 tons' weight. But the fact is that the road will be ready from one end to the other and inaugurated this coming May, thus requiring half the time for completion stated by the commission, while the engineers now declare that it can easily handle 60,000 tons of merchandise annually.

While the railway was being finished, European establishments of one kind and another began to spring up on all sides. Trees supplanted brushwood. From year to year new steamboats, carried up overland, piece by piece on the backs of men, were put together on the Upper Kongo. Commercial agencies were set up on every hand, while Catholic and Protestant missionaries divided the country among them up as high as Tanganyika.

A few figures will give a more striking and exact idea of the present situation on the Kongo. There are now forty-five steamers constantly plying on the waters of the Upper Kongo and its affluents, transporting merchandise, food, and troops, thus carrying life and progress everywhere. It is true that the largest of them are of only forty-five tons burden, for, as has already been said, they had to be brought up from the coast on the backs of men. But now, thanks to the railway, a steamer of 250 tons has reached the Pool, where it will be at work in two months more. Another of the same capacity is now being built at Antwerp, and will join its sister in due time.

What do these steamers carry? All those products collected since the fourteenth century till now only along the coasts of Africa,—ivory, gums, resin, wax, incense, ostrich feathers, pepper, coffee, cocoa, tobacco, cotton, rubber, skins, oils, indigo, fruits, animals of various kinds, etc. To give an idea of what may be exported from the Kongo, I may state that the coffee and cocoa fields planted only in 1891 now contain 1,500,000 coffee plants and 200,000 cocoa plants. Not 100 pounds of rubber was exported in 1885, whereas not less than 3,000,000 pounds were extracted from the forests of the Upper Kongo in 1896, valued at $1,500,000. In 1897 these figures were doubled, and coming years will see them still further increased. It is not astonishing, therefore, that Antwerp tends to become for rubber — as it is already for ivory — the most important market in the world. The following table showing, in round numbers, the trade of the Kongo Independent State, speaks for itself:

Year.	Imports.	Exports.	Totals.
1893 . . .	$2,029,700	$1,503,000	$3,532,700
1894 . . .	2,371,000	2,206,000	4,577,000
1895 . . .	2,368,000	2,427,000	4,795,000
1896 . . .	3,208,000	3,012,000	6,222,000

The figures for 1897 are not yet given out, but it is known that the total surpasses $7,000,000.

A few more figures: In 1891 the Kongo budget was, in round numbers, $911,000. In 1898 it is $3,450,000, with a growing tendency to balance. The number of Europeans on the Kongo is 1,600, of whom 150 are Catholic missionaries and 250 Protestant missionaries. These missionaries occupy some hundred missions scattered over the whole territory, and nobody denies the good they are doing. Among the more important religious establishments should be particularly mentioned the Colonial School, where the State receives abandoned children, and gives them professional and agricultural instruction.

Order is preserved by a remarkable colonial force, whose soldiers are at the same time labourers. This body, which in 1889 contained only 111 natives, now has enrolled 12,000, of whom 8,000 are militiamen and 4,000 volunteers. There are properly constituted courts in all the chief centres, and post-offices all the way to Tanganyika. A telegraphic line is being built from Stanley Pool to Stanley Falls. Lines

for new railways are being examined, so
that in the near future roads will run to
the Nile in one direction, and to Tanganyika and Nyassa in the other. Well-
fitted-out scientific expeditions are study-
ing all the unexplored regions.

Such, rapidly told, is the present condition of the Kongo State, whose participation at the Brussels Exhibition last year
produced a sensation in Europe. The
preparations for the Paris Exhibition of
1900 are already under way on the Kongo,
and on that occasion Europe will, I feel
sure, again proclaim that the constitution
and development of the Kongo State is,
and will remain, one of the brightest jew-
els of the Belgian crown. An uninterrupted series of successes of a scientific,
economic, moral, and military nature; the
bringing within the boundaries of civilisation the whole heart of Africa; the
suppression throughout this immense territory of those cruel bands that used to
send to European markets ivory stolen
through the blood of men, and to Eastern
harems violated orphans; the establish-

ment of order, justice, labour; the faith revealed to millions of human beings, — such are some of the results attained by the Kongo State.

The black population of the Kongo basin is estimated to be 30,000,000 souls. The Belgians have undertaken the task to act as their educators, for the climate will not permit the white man to labour uninterruptedly on the Kongo. He can only direct others. The high table-lands of the Katanga, where the temperature is lower, can become the regions habitable by our race. At present Europeans must return home after a sojourn of two or three years in Africa. The number is continually increasing of those who go back for the fourth and fifth time. In a word, this distant colony has put fresh life into the Belgian nation, which was in danger of growing torpid after sixty years of peace. It needed this new venture to bring out once more its virile qualities.

ENGLAND, THE SÛDAN, AND FRANCE.

ENGLAND, THE SÛDAN, AND FRANCE.

BY HENRY NORMAN,

Editor of the London " Daily Chronicle."

WHERE the Atbara flows into the Nile, 1,530 miles from Cairo, 170 miles from Khartûm, savagery is making to-day its last attempt but one to withstand civilisation in Egypt. The world is necessarily always interested in such conflicts; but this one possesses far more than the usual significance of fights between white men and black. Civilisation has never presented a higher form than the work of England in Egypt, and savagery has never assumed a more hideous aspect than in the Khalifa Abdullah and his Baggara horde. No history appeals more vividly to the imagination of mankind than that upon which the Sphinx for so many centuries has "stared with mysterious, solemn, stony eyes;" and no

problem of to-day involves such incalcu-
lable uncertainties and such colossal possibilities in the relations of all the European
nations to one another as that connected
with the present domination of Great
Britain upon the Nile. All the elements
of a thrilling world-melodrama are present, and the curtain rises to-day upon the
last act. It is well at such a moment to
cast a glance backward and forward.

Everybody remembers how England
came to occupy Egypt in 1882, in con-
sequence of the rebellion of Arabi; how
she invited France to join her, and how
France declined; how she then undertook
the rehabilitation of Egypt single-handed;
how the Mahdi Mohammed Ahmed, first
an Egyptian civil servant, then a slave-
trader at his birthplace, Dongola, raised
the Eastern Sûdan in 1882, isolated the
Austrian, Edward Schnitzler, otherwise
Emin Pasha, in the Equatorial Provinces,
seized El Obeid, the capital of Kordofan,
annihilated the Egyptian Army sent
against him under Hicks Pasha in 1883,
and finally captured Khartûm and slew

Gordon in 1885, thus becoming undisputed master of Upper Egypt. Hicks was doomed to destruction from the start. His "army" was a rabble of cowardly Egyptians, sent to the front in chains. O'Donovan, of Merv, the brilliant correspondent of the "Daily News," said in his last letter that he should shortly be lying in the desert with "a spear-head as big as a shovel" through him, — a prophecy fulfilled to the letter. The mission of Gordon had hardly better prospects. A man of heroic courage and singular virtue, in his relations with other men he could often hardly be described as sane. His personal momentary inspirations and intuitions constituted his rule of life, to the neglect of such mundane considerations as orders from his superiors and his own undertakings. Sent formally "as a man of peace, on a mission of peace," and officially forewarned that he would not be supported by an armed force, he was not long at Khartûm before he began telegraphing minute instructions for an army to be sent to him; and not only that, but his own requests telegraphed in the morning were cancelled by his despatches of the afternoon, till the authorities at Cairo were wholly at a loss to know what line of action to follow. He could have retired from Khartûm when the situation was known to be hopeless; and if he had taken ordinary precautions in keeping the military *enceinte* of Khartûm in repair, he could have held out till the British relief expedition reached him. Ethically, his character commands profound respect; but from another point of view, the story of his career, if ever British opinion permits it to be written, will materially modify the legend which has grown up around him. With his death, the Sûdan lapsed into barbarism, wholly beyond the power of Egypt at that time to destroy. Lord Cromer (then Sir Evelyn Baring) settled down to the gigantic task of bringing back Egypt, ruined by the inconceivable extravagances of the Khedive Ismail, and sucked dry by the concession-hunters and scoundrelly parasites of every European nation, to solvency and military efficiency,

—a task greater and more brilliantly accomplished than any of our time. Then Egypt ended at Wady Halfa. Beyond that was hell, the unimaginable horrors of which have only been fully revealed of late in the narratives of the Mahdi's escaped prisoners, Ohrwalder and Slatin. Beyond Halfa was the little advanced post of Sarras; and I well remember standing in its gate one morning in February, 1892, and, as I had just been present at manœuvres of the Egyptian Army, and had marvelled at the transformation wrought by English officers out of the horde of human sheep, like those who had turned up their throats to the butchers of El Obeid, wondering if the time had not come for the Egyptian flag and the Union Jack to advance once more across the " Belly of Stones " in front of me, which divides Egypt from the Sûdan. On my return I advocated taking the first step, writing as follows : —

" There would be no need to strike the blow at once. A comparatively small addition need be made to the present Egyptian army to enable an amply sufficient force to advance to Dongola, and hold that and the line of communications with Wady Halfa. This single step would bring many waverers at once from the enemy. A pause then would enable that portion of the Sûdan to settle down into peaceful development before another step was taken. Then a farther advance to the next most convenient place might be easily, leisurely, and irresistibly made."[1]

Four years passed; but then the plan I had thus hoped to see was precisely followed. On March 13th, 1896, the Sirdar of the Egyptian Army, Sir Herbert Kitchener, was ordered by the British Government to retake Dongola; on September 26th the Egyptian flag was raised upon the old Mudir's house there; the expedition then stopped, and the British regiment returned to Cairo. On July 13th, 1897, the advance was resumed; Abu Hamed was taken on August 7th, and Berber occupied on September 8th. Kassala was ceded to Egypt by Italy on December 25th, and three Dervish forts in

[1] "Contemporary Review," April, 1892.

the direction of Khartûm were captured
immediately afterward. Two days ago
(March 20th) the entire Egyptian and
British force, the latter greatly strengthened, marched again, and to-day it is
probably fighting the Khalifa's forces under the Emirs Mahmûd and Osman Digna
on the Atbara River. The result needs
no foretelling.

The coming engagement has been described in the telegrams as a "decisive
battle." This it cannot be; the real battle
will be at Omdurman, about the beginning
of August. The present Dervish advance
is due either to the Khalifa's increasing
difficulty in finding food for his forces, or
more probably to his defective information. He no doubt imagines that the advancing force is a small column, chiefly
composed of Egyptian troops, for whom
he has a profound contempt, and whom
he expects to cut to pieces by falling upon
them suddenly, or to isolate by taking
Berber in their rear. His main body will
certainly not fight until it is attacked at
Omdurman (Khartûm, of course, was long

ago abandoned, and is in ruins), which place he has been fortifying for a long time. On his side, the Sirdar will certainly not advance farther until the Nile rises, when his transport can be by river, and the gunboats can lend him their tremendous aid. One steamer carries as much baggage and forage as a thousand camels. It is high Nile at Khartûm in August, and the Sirdar's advance will begin about the middle of July. By that time the railway, now eighty miles north of Berber, will have reached the Nile just below the Atbara. If he does not ask for more white troops, the strength of his army will be approximately as follows: Six battalions of Egyptian infantry, six battalions of Sûdanese infantry, seven squadrons of Egyptian cavalry, the Egyptian Camel Corps, 800 strong, and three field batteries of Egyptian artillery, — a total strength of about 10,000 men, all, of course, under British officers; one battalion each of the Warwickshire Regiment, the Lincolnshire Regiment, the Cameron Highlanders, and the Seaforth Highland-

ers, and a British battery of machine guns,
—a total British force of about 3,500 men.
Against him he will have an army of, perhaps, 60,000 Dervish troops, known to
have not more than 12,000 rifles, composed partly of black soldiers, driven to
battle at the point of the sword, but de-
pending chiefly for its fighting strength
upon the Baggara tribe. In former struggles he has had other formidable Arab
tribes upon his side, — the Jaalin, the
Hadendoa, and the Beni Amer; but these
have now come over to the Egyptian flag,
as their territories have been gradually
reoccupied. Nobody but the Baggara
Arabs fights for the Khalifa an hour after
it is possible to escape from his ven-
geance. These Baggaras, however, are
among the most terrible foes in the
world; they are now at bay, and they
will probably die almost to a man in defence of their last stronghold. Mr. E. F.
Knight, the special correspondent of "The
Times" in the Sûdan, has recently given
a striking picture of these men and their
position. He says : —

"Whatever the Baggara may have been in former days, these last fifteen years of indulgence in unbridled cruelty and rapine have made of them a race of men apart, more like wild beasts, indeed, than men, the enemies of mankind. Sullenly ferocious, having no joy save in slaughter, they seem to have lost the attributes of human nature. They are devoid of all affection for their wives, who are to them of far less account than their cattle. As our surgeons who have tended their wounded in hospital can testify, the Baggara, unlike others of our Dervish foemen, have absolutely no sense of gratitude, and scowl with hatred on those who bring them succour. When lying maimed on the battle-field, they have often treacherously stabbed those who in pity have carried water to their parched lips. They have never shown mercy, and they are now likely to receive little from the tribes which they have ground down with such unspeakable cruelty, and which are now rising, one after the other, all round the doomed Baggara hosts at Omdurman and Metamneh."

Omdurman, therefore, will not be taken without a severe struggle. Taken, however, it will be, and the Dervish power be broken forever, always supposing that

no European or far Eastern complication
necessitates the return of the British
troops, in which case the Egyptian Army
would confine itself to holding Berber.
Remnants of the Dervishes will make
their way up the Nile, or scatter to the
southwest, to be absorbed or destroyed by
the native populations, or be exterminated
piecemeal as the Egyptian administration
gradually extends over the remoter provinces.   For, of course, Omdurman is not
the goal.   "Cape to Cairo" is the ideal,
although at present it is difficult to see
how the through route is to be secured.
But the Equatorial Provinces — Kordofan,
Sennaar, Darfûr, and the Bahr-el-Ghazal
— were all part of the old Egyptian Sûdan,
and they will be restored to the new one.
Omdurman will be held as a fortified base
and centre, and sooner or later a farther
series of advances will be made.   In this
direction, however, the British Government has suffered a most severe disappointment in the revolt in Uganda and
the ruin of Major Macdonald's plan.
Though not officially announced, it was

well known to students of the situation
that an advance down the Nile northward
was to be made *pari passu* with the advance southward from Omdurman. Now
the movement from the south has been
indefinitely postponed, while the French
are straining every nerve to reach the
Upper Nile first. Possibly with a view
to filling the gap in their preparations
left by the wholly unexpected collapse in
Uganda, the Foreign Office consented to
a private expedition attempting a short
cut to the Nile, across the country to the
south of Abyssinia. This was planned by
Mr. S. H. S. Cavendish, a very young,
wealthy, and plucky relative of the Duke
of Devonshire, who has recently returned
from a long, adventurous, and highly successful hunting expedition in Africa. His
preparations were made, a very large sum
of money spent, several officers given leave
to accompany him, his transport engaged,
and a ship sent out from England with his
stores, when suddenly the authorities with-
drew their permission. The reason has
not been made public, and, indeed, all the

details about the Cavendish expedition
are confidential; but it may be surmised
either that they had good reason to fear
complications with the Emperor Menelek
of Abyssinia, or that they have learned .
that the French have already reached the
Nile. Be that as it may, Mr. Cavendish
remains in London, and Indian troops are
marching to suppress the Uganda revolt.
In this connection, too, Lord Salisbury's
warning against the use of small-scale
maps should be borne in mind, and the
fact realised that Khartûm is just about
halfway — 1,700 miles — between Cairo
and the great African lakes.

So far all is plain forecast. The complication and uncertainty come in when
we consider the action of France. Herein
lies not only the gravest problem for
Egypt, but a very real danger to the
peace of Europe. In 1895 it became
known that French expeditions were se-
cretly advancing from the West Coast of
Africa toward the Nile. Sir Edward Grey,
then Under-Secretary for Foreign Affairs,
declared in the House of Commons that

the valley of the Upper Nile was included in the "British and Egyptian Spheres of Influence," and he added that "any advance into the Nile Valley on the part of France would be an unfriendly act; and it was well known to the French Government that we should so regard it." Diplomacy affords no more serious language than this, and the speech produced a deep impression, Mr. Chamberlain, on behalf of the Opposition, expressing entire concurrence. The present Government, I happen to know, maintains precisely the opinion thus expressed by Sir Edward Grey on behalf of Lord Rosebery. The French answer has been to push on her expeditions with redoubled vigour, and to allow it to be frankly declared that their object was "to reach the Upper Nile before the English, and, after reassuring the Mahdi concerning the pacific intentions of France (!), to take possession of the Sûdanese province of Bahr-el-Ghazal." Two expeditions are on their way from the west, under Captain Marchand and Captain Liotard, while a third, under the

Marquis de Bonchamps, comprising five Frenchmen and 500 Abyssinian soldiers, has crossed Abyssinia from the East Coast. The rendezvous of the three parties was Fashoda, an important fortified town on the White Nile, 344 miles from Khartûm, the river being navigable between the two places. Above Fashoda it is choked by enormous masses of floating vegetation. . It is known that Marchand and Liotard reached Dem Soliman and Jur Ghattas in September last,— places in the Bahr-el-Ghazal respectively 300 and 200 miles from Meshra-er-Rek, the "port" of the province, whence the Nile may be reached by water. At this time the Marquis de Bonchamps had reached the Abyssinian boundary of the Sûdan. It has since been repeatedly alleged, on the one hand, that disaster has overtaken the French expeditions, and on the other that they have all three met, as arranged, at Fashoda. The two from the Kongo side, at least, were safe and well on August 22d and September 12th, for private letters bearing these dates were received from

them. Thus France, wholly disregarding
the British protest and warning, has com-
mitted the "unfriendly act" which Great
Britain is pledged to resist.

The case on each side is simple.
France claims that as the Egyptian Government was driven out of the Sûdan by
force of arms, that territory became the
right of any nation which could first re-
occupy it, all previous sovereignty being
at an end. England, for Egypt, replies
that, although the Egyptian forces were
driven out by a revolt, Egypt has never
abandoned her rights there, but has cease-
lessly prepared herself for the re-establish-
ment of her authority. That the whole
of the Sûdan was administered by Egypt
is beyond question. When Gordon was
Governor-General, his steamers went up
and down to Fashoda, and he himself
once went to Bahr-el-Ghazal, and declared
that if he could have a free hand to deal
with it, he would guarantee to pay all the
expenses of the Sûdan. On her own behalf, England adds that, as Egypt evacu-
ated the Sûdan on British advice, Great

Britain is in honour bound to see that she returns to it. Moreover, these southern provinces are the richest in men and products. The Bahr-el-Ghazal is, perhaps, the finest recruiting ground in Africa, and Sennaar is "the granary of the Sûdan." Therefore the Sûdan cannot be successfully administered without them. Finally, as the very life of all Egypt, down to the sea, depends upon the Nile and its periodical rise, it would be fatal to Egypt for any foreign and hostile Power to be seated upon the Upper Nile, where modern engineering skill could draw off its waters for irrigating purposes, and thus instantly ruin whole districts of Lower Egypt.

The coming conquest of Khartûm — one uses the old word, although the old place no longer exists — will, therefore, bring to a head another acute ground of difference between England and France, whose relations are already severely strained by the situation in West Africa. With two such bones of contention as the Nile and the Niger, anything may happen. It can be regarded as perfectly certain that England will not give way so far as the Nile is concerned. Whether France will do so or not, supposing her expeditions to have accomplished their extremely difficult task, remains to be seen. If not, she will open up the whole question of the ultimate fate of Egypt, with which the fate of Turkey, the suzerain of Egypt, is inextricably bound up, and thus precipitate a European situation in which a war between herself and England would be only an incident.

Thus, as I said at the beginning, the march of the white men round the Union Jack, and the black men round the Egyptian crescent and star across the desert to-day, to meet and destroy the horsemen and the riflemen and the spearmen of the accursed Abdullah, deserves attention not only as a long stride of civilisation, but also because it is pregnant with issues of unimaginable gravity for the world.

THE FUTURE OF NIGERIA.

THE FUTURE OF NIGERIA.

BY SIR GEORGE TAUBMAN-GOLDIE,
K.C.M.G.,
Governor of the Royal Niger Company.

THE Niger Territories is the official
name of the sphere acquired for
Great Britain by the Royal Niger Company, and governed by it under Royal
Charter. Within the last few months a
shorter and more picturesque name has
been given by the press to these territories, and has been generally adopted by
the public, — Nigeria. The British sphere
of Nigeria is divided, roughly speaking,
into two sections, as widely separated in
laws, government, customs, and general
ideas about life, both in this world and
the next, as England is from China. Endless misconceptions have arisen from
neglect of this fact, some writers having
discussed Nigeria as if it were entirely
composed of tribes similar to those of the
Lower Niger, or in other West Coast

possessions of Great Britain, while some
writers have treated it as if it were
entirely composed of organised and
semi-civilised Mohammedan States. The
southern third of Nigeria, lying on either
side of the Lower Niger, and to the south
of the river Binue, is for the most part
occupied only by pagans, occupying as
yet only a low rank of civilisation. They
are divided into hundreds of tribes, most
of which, before the advent of British
power, were not only addicted to practices
of outrageous cruelty, but were also constantly warring against each other, chiefly
for the purpose of capturing slaves. This
southern third of Nigeria — and especially
the maritime and most barbarous portion
— has naturally been more frequently visited by Europeans than the regions of the
far interior, so that to many persons the
word Niger conjures up only a picture of
mangrove swamps and tropical forests,
inhabited by semi-nude savages living
under the terrors and horrors resulting
from witchcraft and fetishism.

I do not propose to say much about

this southern third of Nigeria, because, although the forests teem with valuable products, such as rubber, and there seems little doubt that the trade of this region, in forest products alone, will at no distant time attain such dimensions as to count materially in the volume of trade of the British Empire, a considerable period must elapse before these inferior tribes, who have doubtless been gradually driven south toward the sea by the pressure of higher races advancing from the north, acquire the industrious habits on which alone a wealthy and civilised State can be built up. To most of this region applies the popular idea of the negro as a somewhat indolent person, with moderate wants and little ambition.

Very different, however, are the conditions of the inland two thirds of Nigeria lying between the Great Sahara on the north and the two great branches of the rivers Niger and Binue on the south. This region covers the larger portion of the Central Sûdan. It is specially important to bear in mind its Sûdanese charac-

ter, at a time when the attention given by
the press to Egyptian questions tends to
confine to the eastern or Egyptian Sûdan
a name which, as every geographer knows,
applies to all the black man's lands under
Moslem influence. The Sûdan extends
some 3,000 miles across Africa from the
frontiers of Abyssinia on the east to those
of Senegal on the west. No adequate
policy can be formed for dealing with the
northern two thirds of Nigeria without
due recognition of its close connection
with other Sûdanese regions, — a connection due partly to unity of religion, and
partly to the constant intercommunication
maintained by the streams of Hausa caravans, bent on trade or pilgrimage, or both
combined, which flow from Kano and
other great cities of Hausaland into almost every part of Africa north of the
equator. To this larger, more important,
and more interesting part of Nigeria, I
wish to draw special attention.

For the sake of brevity, it is desirable
to find an appropriate name for the whole
of the Sûdanese region, and I know of

none more suitable than that often given
to it, — Hausaland. It is true that in
considerable districts — for instance, in
Northern Nupe — the inhabitants are not
Hausas, but have a language of their
own; yet even in these portions the civilised habits and modes of thought of the
Hausas are predominant. The caravans
which pass almost continuously along
the bush-tracks in every direction are
Hausa. The merchants in the towns are
Hausa, and the *lingua franca* is the Hausa
tongue. But the Hausas are not rulers,
even in their own provinces. Supreme
political power in Hausaland is held by
the Fulah race, — an alien people of uncer-
tain, but probably Eastern origin, who, in
the early part of this century, conquered
the seven old Hausa kingdoms, whence
they gradually extended their power
southward and eastward, thus forming the
vast empire known as Sokoto Gandu, or,
more briefly, as the Fulah Empire. The
Fulahs, when of pure breed, have light
complexions, regular and fine features,
and oval faces; and some of the women

are possessed of striking beauty, both of
face and figure. But as Fulah men frequently intermarry with women of Hausa
and other African races, many of the rul-
ing caste are now of negro colour and feature. The conquest of the immense and
fairly civilised populations of Hausaland
at the beginning of this century, by a
comparatively small number of Fulahs,
has often excited surprise. The Fulahs
are undoubtedly inferior to the Hausas
in the arts of peace, and, so far as it is
known, they have not introduced any single element of civilisation into Hausaland,
while their passion for slave raiding has
impoverished and depopulated those regions. Their military success has been,
doubtless, due to religious fanaticism and
to personal courage. To these qualifica-
tions of the Fulahs of fanatical and first-
class fighting men must be added their
astuteness as diplomatists and their
knowledge how to "divide and govern."
The proud character of the race is well
described by the proverbial saying that a
Fulah man slave will escape or kill his

master, and that a Fulah girl slave will rule the harem or die.

But the main secrets of the Fulah conquests and of their present power is the fact of their being an equestrian race. Their cavalry, armed like our own with lances and swords, is formidable to disciplined troops, and is irresistible against an untrained army on foot. History tells us that this rule has been universal. The part played by the horse in the conquest of Mexico by Cortes is too well known to need more than a passing reference; so, too, in Europe, mere handfuls of knights used to put to flight masses of sturdy *villeins*, until Morgarten and Crécy showed how disciplined infantry could resist cavalry. The thorough training and leading of Hausa soldiers by British officers and the introduction of modern artillery into the Sûdan regions have commenced, and will, before long, complete the enfranchisement of Hausaland from the unceasing slave-raiding which has been so terribly destructive to human life and an absolute barrier to prosperity.

This summary of the political and social situation in Hausaland has been necessary, because misgovernment has been the main obstacle to progress there. At the International Geographical Congress, two years ago, Sir John Kirk very aptly described tropical Africa as "a lost continent, owing to the misrule which has pervaded it." His description is true of all tropical Africa; but it is specially true of Hausaland, where, but for native misgovernment, all the elements of a great civilisation are present. The Hausas are possessed of remarkable energy, judgment, and intelligence. They are skilful and almost artistic workers in metals, leather, and other materials. They possess histories, songs, and tales written in their own tongue. Stanley says that of all the African races the Hausa alone valued a book. They have the advantage of a fertile soil, and they display that eager desire to get on in the world which is so unpleasing in the individual but so valuable for the State. Above all, they are unlike most African races in that they

are extremely industrious, notwithstanding
the little inducement to display this virtue
in a land where the acquisition of wealth
has too frequently led to loss of liberty or
life. Many competent authorities have,
accordingly, declared Hausaland to be by
far the most valuable section of tropical
Africa.

For excellent reasons, its mineral resources have not yet been explored,
although some deposits are already known
to exist. In this connection it is well to
remember that only thirty to forty years
ago the immense mineral wealth of South
Africa was so little suspected that a considerable section of the English press used
to advocate retirement from South Africa,
excepting Cape Town, which was to be
held as a coaling station on the road to
India. But although minerals are most
valuable to give a start to a new country,
the only foundations of permanent prosperity are the industry, intelligence, and
prolificness of its inhabitants combined
with fertility of soil. All these conditions
are united in Hausaland. The manner in

which population there rights itself after the wholesale destruction resulting from slave raids is hardly credible in colder climates where infancy is prolonged, while at least six times the existing population could support themselves in comfort. If properly administered, Hausaland would, at no distant date, become as valuable as any equal area of British India; but patience is needed.

The vital question to consider is how to maintain and increase British power there pending the final pacification of the country and the consequent development of a revenue sufficient to support normal colonial administration. The initial labours of opening up Nigeria and of laying the foundation of British justice there have so far been successful. The bugbear of Fulah power, which the official documents of ten years ago declared would crush the Niger Company at the first impact, has been, at any rate partially, laid by the recent campaign. The international struggles of the last fifteen years, with France and then Germany and then again

France, have been gradually reduced to modest proportions. The most cogent motives for absolute silence have ceased. It seems to me the time has come to discuss publicly the methods calculated to lead to success as well as those certain to lead to failure.

In discussing this subject I am confronted with a personal difficulty. Being connected with the company which governs Nigeria, it may be thought that my views are necessarily prejudiced. Let me, then, briefly state, once for all, that I have no mandate from the Niger Company, that the views advanced are purely personal, that these views are consistent either with the continuance of the company or its disappearance, and that I shall place myself at an entirely outside standpoint.

Great Britain is at present in a hot fit of empire-making, which, like African fever, has its alternation of cold fits; so lately as 1865 the House of Commons Select Committee, appointed to examine into West African matters, reported as follows: " That all further extension of territory, or assumption of government, or new treaties offering any protection to native tribes, would be inexpedient." It was, perhaps, partly due to this resolution that, until the Royal Niger Company stepped in and acquired half a million square miles of the most valuable part of tropical Africa, not a single step was taken into the interior by any of the West African colonies, which allowed another colonising Power to hem them in to the sea and deprive them of their hinterland. If a few failures and disasters, such as must occasionally occur in building up empire, were to happen, we should probably see the same policy revived. If the quondam author of " Greater Britain " urges our retirement to coast spheres in Africa at a time when colonial expansion is at fever heat, what will others of his opinion say — and do, if in power — when, as must inevitably happen, temporary misfortunes and disappointments occur, when reaction succeeds the outburst of energy displayed since Germany commenced as a colonising Power, and when the watchword, "*Imperium et libertas!*" gives way to the "Rest and be thankful" against which we used to chafe twenty to thirty years ago? There would be little chance, in such circumstances, of Parliament continuing the financial support which would certainly be required by Nigeria during its infancy, to maintain the costly method of normal imperial government. The inevitable result would be failure, disappointment, and abandonment. Assuming that enough has been said to show the necessity of continuing in some shape or other the existing abnormal system which has enabled Nigeria to pay its way without the assistance of a single shilling from the Imperial Government, the next point to consider is how much of this is essential.

The only vital condition to my mind is that Nigeria should continue to be administered as heretofore by a permanent council, untrammelled by bureaucratic formulæ, experienced in African questions, corresponding somewhat with the Council of the Governor-General of India, controlled, as are both chartered companies and governors of Crown colonies, by a Secretary of State, but no more subject than British India is to constant parliamentary interference, and above all administering not locally, like Crown colonies, but from home, as the Council of the Niger Company has always done. The permanence of the members of such a council, subject, of course, to changes made by the Secretary of State, seems to me to be of vital importance. Let me say, with all respect, that I look on the appointment of the present Secretary of State for the Colonies as likely to mislead the public mind in regard to the principles for dealing with inner African dependencies. Mr. Chamberlain's extraordinary vigour, rapidity, voracity for work, and willingness to accept responsibility before Parliament, are likely to give the Colonial Office a reputation of suitability for creative administration which cannot be expected to survive his tenure of that particular office.

The second vital point is that the Ad-

ministrative Council should govern from
home and not locally in Nigeria. This
is the only possible way of securing continuity of administration of a region where
no local continuity can be obtained at
present, owing to the nature of the climate,
in which Nigeria has perhaps greater difficulties to meet than the other European
possessions in Equatorial Africa to which
I have referred. There are, indeed, high
ranges of plateaux in the far interior
where white administrators could retain
their activity and powers of work for long
periods; but these areas of the Central
Sudan are not yet effectively occupied,
so that for some years to come they must
be left out of account. Yet I desire to
draw attention to them, as they will
afford the ultimate solution of the difficult question of the administration of
Nigeria.

Meanwhile it must be taken for granted
that no local continuity of government is
at present practicable, and this in regions
where continuity is of vital importance,
owing to the enormous difficulties to be

overcome. In the coast possessions of West Africa, where European administrators and traders live on or near the seaboard, and are practically under the protection of the Imperial Navy, and where powerful native governments do not exist, or can be dealt with by Imperial troops, as in the Ashanti War of 1874, local administration is not open to the same objections, although it is well known that the Colonial Office is compelled to exercise a larger share in the actual government of West African colonies than it does in Crown colonies in healthier climates, where continuity of local government can be maintained.

In Nigeria, ever since the issue of the charter, the two agents-general, or local heads of the Niger Government, have been only executive officers with considerable latitude in carrying out their instructions, and they relieve each other at short intervals, to allow of their renewing their vigour at home. The real work of the administration, the work performed by governors — or by governors and councils — in

Nigeria. 183

Crown colonies or by the council of the
Governor-General in India, has been dealt
with day by day by a council living in the
temperate and healthy climate of London,
where not only can men work continuously
for twice as many hours a day as they
can in West Africa, — a vital matter in an
emergency, — but where the character and
effectiveness of the work done is entirely
different.   To this system, and not to any
individual merit, has been due the successful administration to which both Lord
Salisbury and Lord Kimberly have borne
such striking and gratifying testimony.

Whether this system continues as heretofore under the Chartered Niger Company,
or whether, that company retiring from
Nigeria, a governing council is created
ad hoc, is only an accidental, I do not say
unimportant feature.

The one essential element is that continuity shall be maintained by permanent,
unwearying, and bold administration from
home as heretofore controlled, but not
conducted, by the office of a Secretary of
State, until the simlas of Hausaland, to

which I have already alluded, are occupied and utilised, and a sufficient volume of commerce, and therefore revenue, is created to permit local government of the Norman type. When that day arrives, the foundations of Nigeria will have been fully laid, and it may then be left to natural causes to raise that great structure of Nigerian prosperity which I shall not see, but in which, under reasonable conditions, I have the most absolute faith.

THE KINGDOM OF UGANDA.

THE KINGDOM OF UGANDA.

BY COLONEL F. D. LUGARD,

Commander of English Forces in Eigeria, Formerly of Uganda.

THE people of Uganda are a Bantu race, much intermixed with the Wahuma stock. The latter are a great pastoral, nomad tribe, who probably form one of the most important offshoots of the stock from whence sprang the Abyssinians, Somalis, Gallas, and other powerful tribes, distinguished from the Bantu races not merely by their aquiline and regular features, their thin lips, and the fact that they have curly *hair* instead of the *wool* of the negroid races, but also by the different construction of their languages. The Wahuma, it is related, conquered the countries lying to the west of the Victoria Nyanza, including Uganda, Unyoro, Toru, Ankoli, Karagwe, and toward the Lake Tanganyika. They still retain Ankoli and Toru in the British sphere. This vast kingdom was known under the name of Kitara.

Since there are no written records of the past, it is difficult to learn anything reliable concerning the ancient history of the Waganda. Emin Pasha, Dr. Felkin, the Rev. C. T. Wilson, and other early residents in and around the country have collected much interesting information, which is easily accessible to those who care to learn more of these people. Coming, however, to the events of to-day and the people as we find them at the present time, it is the unanimous verdict of every one, without exception, who has been brought into contact with this remarkable race, that they show a most extraordinary advance upon all the people who surround their country for thousands of miles to north, south, east, or west. They have, in fact, a certain civilisation of their own, a wonderful intelligence, customs, tradition, etiquettes innumerable, and a wonderfully comprehensive language with an enormous vocabulary, which alone indicates the superiority of their intellectual attainments and the range of their ideas, as contrasted with the crude and simple dialects of their neighbours. Their qualities of disposition are marked. They are an extremely brave race, though treacherous from our point of view, are passionately fond of learning, and are capable of high attainments if educated from early childhood.

I reached Uganda in 1891 as the first British officer to enter the country on a political and administrative mission since the time of Gordon and his emissaries, Chaillu, Long, and Emin Pasha. Gordon and his lieutenants had represented the extension of civilisation from the North, and were the representatives of the Khedive and of Egyptian rule. I came as the representative of the Imperial British East African Company, a corporation under royal charter, vested with the delegated powers of sovereignty of the Queen of Great Britain. The rule of the Khedive and the germs of civilisation implanted in the Nile Valley by Baker, and developed by Gordon, had been swept away by the religious upheaval which had enthroned the Mahdi in Omdurman, and placed an iron despotism over the tribes of the Eastern Sûdan. It was the mission of England now to advance from the east, through the vast Sphere of Influence secured to her from Mombasa on the East Coast to the valley of the Nile and its watershed to the west.

At this time I found the country torn by religious dissensions and a prey to anarchy and internecine war. Not the least remarkable of the traits of the Waganda is their passionate devotion to religion, and, like the Athenians of old, their cult is that of " the Unknown God." Mohammedanism taught by Arab missionaries from the East Coast, and Christianity as interpreted by Roman Catholic missionaries of a French Algerian mission, and Protestantism as represented by the English Church Missionary Society were the protagonists on this virgin field, while paganism retained its hold on the more illiterate and less accessible classes of the population. It was indeed a most interesting study, this war of the creeds; and, had the rivalry been confined to an *odium theologicum* only, an administrator might have regarded it with the interest of a philosopher, and, while taking steps to prevent violence and war, have remained a spectator of the struggle, confident, with Carlyle, that that which held the strongest germ of truth within it would ultimately win. But, unfortunately, it was far otherwise.

Though religion had lent its name to the strife, and accentuated its bitterness, the factions had become more political than religious at the time of my arrival. The Christians and pagans were the adherents of Mwanga, who, after various vicissitudes, was now on the throne, while the Mohammedans were for the moment the defeated party, and were massed on the frontier under their Sultan Mbogo, — Mwanga's uncle and rival for the kingship of Uganda, — and in alliance with Kaba Rega, the powerful King of Unyoro. Their constant raids made it essential to deal with them first, and as soon as I

had concluded a treaty with Mwanga and
the chiefs, we marched out to meet them.
It was my intense desire to come to terms
with these people, who comprised a very
large part of the population of Uganda,
and to repatriate them ; but I had not yet
acquired sufficient influence to carry my
point, and my negotiations failed, and we
were compelled to fight.   Some 15,000 to
20,000 combatants were ranged on either
side, and my handful of " Askaris " formed
the centre and rallying points of the so-
called " Christian " army.   We defeated
them.   Later on I made a new attempt,
— its extreme difficulty is described in
my book, — and I am glad to say it was
successful.   The Mohammedans rendered
up their Sultan Mbogo to me, and he
came to reside at Kampala with me.   I
assigned them three small provinces in
which to settle down, and a small proportion of the offices of State.   It is my great
regret that since I left the country this
arrangement has been upset, the Mohammedans have been accused of intrigue
and treachery, and ousted and, I believe,

almost annihilated. I do not doubt the intrigue; it is inevitable and certain in Uganda; but recent events have proved, if further proof were necessary, that intrigue and rebellion were at least as common to the other factions as to this. But to return to our protagonists. At the moment, the factions of the Christians and the pagans were united in their common dread of the Mohammedans; but, this removed, they settled down into a triangular duel. Here again the religious name was merely an accessory to further division of interests. The pagan party, called the *Fublauji*, or Chang-smokers, since they held to the old customs of the country which all three religious factions alike had condemned, were the blind adherents of the King, who was at heart a pagan, and they detested all the religions alike; and the upstarts who had by their religious influence made themselves the chiefs of the country, and superseded the old pagan aristocracy — if that term is admissible.

Their political objects were to get rid

194   The Kingdom

of all Europeans and all the troublesome religions which had proved such a curse to the country. The Christians again were equally divided between themselves, by causes quite apart from religion, though accentuated by it. The Roman Catholics were the French party who, taught by their priests, resented English influence, the more so that it strengthened, in their view, their detested rivals, "the English Party," or Protestants. Such were the promising materials out of which it was the task of the British Administrator to endeavour to evolve law and order, and such the factions between which he had to endeavour to hold the balance evenly and to distribute that justice without partiality which it is the pride of the English-speaking race to carry with them into the far places of the earth, and to which, as Lord Justice Vaughan Williams said the other day,[1] is attributable the success of the English as colonists. Credit — an ephemeral and a worthless credit — may be gained before Europe by the aggran-

[1] *Vide*, the London "Times," February 3d, 1898, p. 10.

disement of the two factions who have
their loud-voiced representatives ready to
sing the praises of the Administrator who
adopts the views of their factions, or to
execrate through the far-reaching chan-
nels of the press of Europe him who will
not listen to and follow their counsels.
But the Mohammedan and the pagan,
who form probably the bulk of the population, and who have no French Colonial
Party, and no English mission enthusiasts
to champion their cause, — are they and
their wives and people therefore to be
"no man's child," and dubbed the "out-
law and criminal classes of Uganda"?
Until their claims to recognition and to
justice are considered equally with the
Christian factions, we shall hear of continual uprisings in Uganda, of discontent,
and of mutiny.

The railway proceeds but slowly; and
when it reaches the vast lake a new era
will dawn, not only for Uganda, but for
Central Africa. The development of the
country will be on no known lines; for
when in the world's history have coun-

tries, in the heart of a till recently unexplored land, and peopled by savages
absolutely devoid of clothes, begun their
march of progress by a ready-made railway 700 miles long ?   This vast stretch of
land, reaching from the sea to the inland
lakes, is for the most part a very beautiful
and a very fertile one.   Its products may
be almost anything that will grow in a
sub-tropical region and a rich soil.   They
will be what the world of commerce needs,
and will be dictated by the wants of civilised man.   Indigenous coffee, fibres of
value, rubber, oil-seeds, and other products
may be quoted ; but where a railway runs
from one of the finest harbours in the
world to the second largest lake on the
planet, it has almost seemed to me idle
to forecast the future commercial possibilities of a country where the soil is rich,
the rainfall abundant, and the altitude
renders the climate very fairly healthy,
even in spite of the known dangers of
virgin soil and virgin forests.

My early connection with the country
has given me the keenest interest in

its present and future. My old friends
among the chiefs still write to me constantly, though it is now six years since I
left them; and I trust that some day
I may see them again, when other duties
permit of it. Meanwhile, I am always
glad to be able to interest any one in a
country which is full of interest, and in
whose future, under proper management,
I believe. I trust, therefore, that these
lines, written under press of much work,
may interest their readers.

ABYSSINIA AND ITS PEOPLE.

ABYSSINIA AND ITS PEOPLE.

BY CAPTAIN T. C. S. SPEEDY,

Member of the Recent British Mission to King Menelek.

UNTIL comparatively lately but little has been known of even the country of Abyssinia. It has been to the other nations of the world almost a *terra incognita*, a somewhat mythical land supposed to be inhabited if not by savages, at any rate by a wholly uncivilised people. Its boundaries even have been often questioned, and the fact that it comprises several distinct nations speaking different languages has perhaps been known to very few. Such, however, is the case. Abyssinia consists of three large provinces, — Tigré on the north, Amhara on the south, and Shoa to the southeast. The people of Tigré speak Ethiopic, and those of Amhara and Shoa, Amharic.

The Emperor of Abyssinia bears in his own country the title of "Negusa Negust," the interpretation of which is "King of Kings," meaning that the reigning sovereign has by his own power conquered and subdued all other chiefs and aspirants to the throne, and that he reigns supreme until some chief greater and more powerful than himself shall arise and dethrone him.

The three sovereigns under whose sway Abyssinia has of late come to the front and attracted the attention of Europe, have been Theodore, who held his court at Magdala, and reigned from 1855 to 1868; Johannes, his successor, 1870 to 1889, whose capital was Makaleh; and the present Emperor Menelek, whose palace is at Adis Adaba, the town in which the late British mission, under Mr. Rennel Rodd, visited him in 1897.

These kings had all a very distinct individuality, and each in his own way was a remarkable man. Theodore, but little understood and much maligned, was a man of great foresight and very advanced ideas; he was extremely anxious to bring his country to the front, and in every way to promote its prosperity. He ardently longed for a seaport, and it was the keen disappointment of finding that he was not aided by the European Powers in these matters that caused his personal downfall and ruin.

Johannes was distinctly more of a warrior than Theodore, with a less keen intellect; and the present Emperor, Menelek, although a man of no mean abilities, is parsimonious, and unwilling to make present outlay for future benefit. He is, however, greatly influenced by his clever wife, Ta-hai-itu, and his Commander-in-Chief, Ras Makonen, both of whom have aims in the right direction for Abyssinia.

The people themselves have all the instincts for civilisation and progress, and their physique is that of a perfectly independent and clear-headed race. They are well formed, the men averaging five feet ten inches in height, with good features, bearing but little if any resemblance to other African tribes, and none to the negro. They are athletic and hardy, having great powers of endurance, the rugged and mountainous nature of their country inducing, from their earliest years, a capability for climbing and rough walking, equalled perhaps only by the Tyrolese. They make excellent soldiers with even a minimum of training, and show an aptitude for following the evolutions of drill which is surprising in an untutored race.

Possessing strong characters and ardent passions, it is at present, in their somewhat lawless condition, difficult to reckon upon their line of action in exceptional circumstances. In cases where their affection and confidence have been gained, they show the most unswerving fidelity, even to the white man, and run risks of punishment from their own chief or emperor rather than betray confidence. It was well known that before the first British expedition to Abyssinia in 1867 and 1868, under Lord Napier, of Magdala, the captives in the dungeons of Magdala were able to send messages to the British agent at Massoua, who procured for them wines, provisions, and money, which their trusty

Abyssinian servants conveyed surreptitiously to them at the risk of their own lives and liberty.

Should, however, no such confidence or affection exist, treachery, cruelty, and deceit are often met with; but even these qualities do not exist among them to a greater extent than among many uncivilised peoples.

But little can be said of the morality of the Abyssinians. This, however, is chiefly attributable to the prevalent form of marriage, which is merely a civil contract of the loosest description, dissolved at the pleasure of either of the contracting parties.

There is besides this a binding and most sacred form of marriage celebrated by the Church, from which there is no divorce; and it is, perhaps, the irrevocability of this tie that causes the bulk of the people to prefer the civil contract, rather than any tendency to gross sensuality. I do not think I have met one in a thousand who had chosen the marriage in church.

The Abyssinians are a Christian nation of ancient date, having been converted to Christianity in the fourth century, by missionaries sent from Alexandria, by Bishop Athanasius, the author of the creed that bears his name.

Their tenets are similar to those of the Coptic Church, and for the last two centuries the "Abuna," or High Priest of Abyssinia, has been a Copt from Egypt. Before leaving for Abyssinia he is invariably obliged to take an oath never to return to his own country. They hold the Divinity of our Lord, the redemption of man, the annunciation to the Virgin Mary; and they believe in Purgatory, but they allow no images in their places of worship.

The walls of their churches are frequently adorned with rude frescos representing the crucifixion, — accurately depicting the thieves on either side, the Roman soldier offering a sponge filled with vinegar on the end of a spear, and the Mother of our Lord at the foot of the cross. Other paintings depict the passage of the Red Sea, the soldiers being armed with match-locks, Eve offering the forbidden fruit to Adam in the shape of a huge banana, and many different scenes from Scripture history. They also introduce the likenesses of their favourite saints, — Saint George and the Dragon, Saint George being, curiously enough, the patron saint of the country. They are extremely tenacious of their faith, and in the sixteenth century, when the country was overrun and subdued by Moslems from the Adal Kingdom on the east, now known as Somaliland, they preferred death to the abnegation of Christianity. Messages imploring assistance were surreptitiously sent to Portugal, and an armed force, under Cristoforo de Gama, enabled them to reclaim their country from the infidel invaders, since which time they have remained in undisturbed possession of their Christian faith.

The laws of Abyssinia are primitive, and based on those of the Israelites, "An eye for an eye." There are neither law courts nor lawyers; both plantiff and defendant plead their own cause. Formerly, prior to the appointment by King Theodore of executioners, the guilty person, in case of murder, was slain in exactly the same manner in which he had taken the life of his victim. For instance, if a man killed another with a sword, the avenger of blood had to use a similar weapon. If death had been caused by blows from a club, a club was used to take the life of the murderer. This law most unjustly operated even in cases of man-slaughter; and the life of a man who unwittingly and unintentionally had caused the death of another could be demanded by the relatives of the deceased. Among many others, an instance of this kind was once related to me. Two men were cutting grass on the side of a precipice, and when they were about to descend one of them fastened the end of a rope round his companion's body to lower him down the cliff, and attached the other end to the trunk of a tree. Accidentally, the man to be lowered slipped before all was ready, and a coil of the rope, becoming entangled round his neck, he was strangled. His comrade, on subsequently descending by slipping down the rope, was horrified to find him dead at the bottom, and hastened to the village to report the circumstance. The judge passed a sentence of man-slaughter, and ordered a fine of one hundred and fifty dollars to be paid to the widow. The widow, however, refused the compensation, and demanded the literal carrying out of the law. After some deliberation, it was agreed that she could carry her point, and the unfortunate and perfectly innocent man was sentenced to be hung with the same rope which had caused the fatal accident; the rope was, accordingly, fastened round his waist, and a coil of the same passed round his neck, and he was hauled up a few feet from the ground, suspended a few moments and then lowered again. The widow, believing him from all appearances to be dead, was satisfied; but the relatives of the victim hastened to him and applied restoratives, which were so effective that in course of time he got up and walked away. The widow was furious, and demanded that the sentence should be again enacted, adding: " Next time I will hold on to his feet until he is dead." The judge, however, declared that justice must be tempered with mercy, and her demand was not complied with.

In conducting a lawsuit, the case opens by the plaintiff laying his complaint before the judge. The charge having been heard, a bystander is placed between plaintiff and defendant as "asteraki," — *i. e.*, " peacemaker," — a kind of clerk to keep order between them, and the defendant is directed to reply. After listening for a short time the judge enjoins silence by holding up his hand, and two or more elders, called " Shimagelli," are then appointed to act as jury. The plaintiff is then allowed to go into the details of his case, while the defendant may murmur dissent or denial at intervals by grunts of disapprobation, though no word is allowed. Brevity and speaking to the point are imperatively demanded of both parties.

When the plaintiff has spoken, the defendant is heard, and no interruptions are permitted while either man is speaking.

A curious custom is followed during a lawsuit, which is part of the dramatic habit of the Abyssinians of expressing their feelings by the way in which they wear their clothes. Either plaintiff or defendant may take a corner of the toga, or shammah, worn by the asteraki, and, having knotted it, may hold it up before the judge, and, laying a hand expressively on the knot, may wager that he is speaking the truth. A man will exclaim: " I wager a mule, a sheep, a fat ox, or a jar of honey that my statement is correct;" and if his opponent accepts the wager, he unties the knot, saying: " I accept." Witnesses are then heard; and when the case is ended, judge and jury confer apart, and judgment is given, the loser paying his wager to the judge in lieu of other fee.

The custom already referred to, of expressing their feelings by the manner of arranging their toga, is unique and artistic. This toga is a large white cotton sheet, woven in the country, with a deep red border, at least twelve inches in width, a foot and a half from the edge. To express scorn, a man will take the end of the toga, or "shammah," and raise it to his face, drawing it lightly across his nose just below the eyes, and turn at the same moment with an indignant and haughty gesture from his opponent. The superiority of a chief when conversing with his inferiors in rank is shown by throwing the shammah over both shoulders, crossing it over the left, thereby indicating that no hand of friendship is to be offered. Equality is indicated by the shammah being thrown over the left arm only, leaving the right hand free to greet an acquaintance. Not infrequently when pleading his cause the accused, at the commencement of a trial, will draw his shammah before his face and, with expressions of humility and shame, state his defence, whether guilty or not; at the same time he will whisk one end of it into the semblance of a rope, and, passing it round his neck, exclaim:

" Hang me, if I deserve it," or, twisting it into the likeness of a sword, say: " Behead me, if I speak falsely," then, allowing it to fall to the ground, he will drop on his knee, adding: " But what I ask is justice."

Although the Abyssinians are a decidedly progressive race, and fond of meeting and mixing with other nations, and anxious for commerce and the improvement of their country generally, they are heavily handicapped by their despotic government, and the individual character of their Emperor and various chiefs. From the latter, for instance, they are often subject to exorbitant taxation, so that they have little or no inducement to cultivate their land further than is sufficient for their immediate use, although enough cereals could be grown to form a large export. The soil is principally black clay, excellent for the growth of wheat, barley, oats, millet, and coffee. The latter indeed grows wild everywhere, the plants, at an elevation of from three to five thousand feet, growing twelve feet high and upward. An extensive trade could also be carried on in honey, beeswax, butter, aloes, sulphur, ebony, ox-hides, ivory, and civet-musk. Iron is also common, cropping up all over the country, while gold and copper have frequently been met with.

Another defect which militated against the promotion of commerce is the absence of a seaport. The present Emperor is not anxious to have one. He represents, with some reason, that a port could easily be wrested from him by any nation possessing a fleet, and he has not a sufficiently well-trained army or ordnance that would enable him to hold his own against a maritime power; whereas the high table-land of Abyssinia, with its almost inaccessible fastnesses, renders defence in the interior a comparatively easy matter. On the western border, moreover, lie the inimical Mahdists, who, with their hatred of Christians, are ever ready to harass and oppose any traders from or to their own land. This same foresight caused Theodore to seek the intercession of England and the other European Pow-

ers to grant him a protected passage
to the coast; and though his wish may
have been chimerical, there is no doubt
that the want of such safe transport is
one of the greatest hinderances to the
prosperity and advancement of this little
kingdom. These difficulties make it quite
impossible to form any definite idea of
the influence of Abyssinia in the future
of Africa. Time and the wisdom of their
rulers, combined with European aid, will
alone be able to determine this point; but
there is but little doubt that she possesses
all the capabilities of becoming a very
powerful factor; and it can only be hoped
that in the near future Ethiopia may re-
sume her original position as one of the
great empires of the world.

THE REPUBLIC OF LIBERIA —
ITS FUTURE.

THE REPUBLIC OF LIBERIA — ITS FUTURE

BY J. C. HARTZELL, D.D.,
Missionary Bishop of Africa.

LYING between the fifth and eighth degrees of north latitude, on the West Coast of Africa, is the little Negro Republic of Liberia. Its coast-line is about 300 miles, and its domain extends 250 miles into the interior, so that its territory includes, perhaps, 75,000 square miles. It owes its existence to good men in America, both North and South, who, many years ago, felt that the freed people of the United States should have a place in the land of their fathers where they could have the opportunity and satisfaction of building a nation of their own, which should demonstrate the capacity of the negro for nation-building, and also open the way for his having a share in the civilisation and redemption of the

African continent. The American Colonisation Society, and kindred organisations, inaugurated and have fostered this philanthropic movement by facilitating the migration of negroes from the United States, and by advice and material aid in educational and other enterprises.

There are now in the Republic about 24,000 Americo-Liberians, speaking, of course, the English language; and, perhaps, 1,000,000 native Africans. The former are emigrants from the United States, or their descendants; and the latter are made up of various tribes of aborigines, speaking many dialects, acknowledging the sovereignty of the Republic, but as a whole living in barbarism, as their fathers before them have done for many centuries.

The form of government is modelled after that of the United States, and only negroes can own land, become citizens, or hold office. A few thousand natives have become civilised, and are a part of the nation. For twenty-five years Liberia was a colony, under the immediate direction

of the Colonisation Societies; but in
1847 the nation was formed and received
the friendly recognition and good will of
other nations. Liberia and Hayti are
the only nations in the world controlled
entirely by negroes.

To say that the hopes of the friends of
the negro as a nation-builder have been
realised during the past fifty years in
Liberia, would not be true. On the other
hand, to accept the uncharitable and un-
kind criticisms of the struggling Republic,
which are heard along the coast from
many traders and travellers, and often reit-
erated in Europe and America, would be
doing great injustice to the people of
Liberia. I have recently held conversa-
tions with representative Liberians and
others in the principal centres of the
Republic, and have studied its present conditions and outlook. When we consider
the difficulties which these people have
had to meet in a new and, to many, a
hostile climate, their lack of wealth and experience in government, surrounded and
permeated by multitudes of barbarous

heathen, and subjected constantly to the
uncharitable criticisms of white traders
and travellers, the marvel is that so much
in the way of efficient government and
advance in social conditions has been accomplished. True, their national domain,
rich in minerals and agricultural possibilities, has not even been explored; but it
is also true that, until within a very few
years, but little advance has been made
by other nations on either coast of the
continent in extending practical and efficient government among the natives of
the interior. The advance of the past
few years has been the result of enormous expenditures in money, backed by
powerful Governments, able to command
the best administrative talent.

President Coleman and his official ad-
visers have come fully to realise the increasing difficulties which their nation
must face. In the first place, a few great
nations are rapidly dominating all Africa,
and the possessions of any one small nation on the continent must be in constant
jeopardy unless its Government has the

practical friendship of at least one great nation. Both Germany and France are exceedingly anxious to acquire the territory of the Republic, and France holds a treaty by which, if any part of the Republic's domain is alienated, it will have the right to reassert its claim for certain valuable territories on the coast, and also its hinterland down to within forty miles of the coast, which would mean practically the annihilation of the Republic. Recent troubles between a German subject and some Liberian natives led to the demand for a large indemnity in money and other concessions, accompanied with a proposed treaty for a German Protectorate, which, if agreed to, would settle the dispute.

The growth of the Republic in population is slow, and it cannot be large until, by the opening up of the country, there can be opportunities for the investment of capital, so that remunerative labour and agricultural openings can be given to those who migrate from the United States and elsewhere. Lack of money has made the development of an efficient educational system impossible, and the second generation of children is growing up with but few facilities for instruction.

What Liberia wants and needs is, first, that her nationality shall be guaranteed by some powerful friend. She naturally turns to the United States, and if for any cause a proper protectorate cannot be secured from that source, she next turns to England. Both nations have shown her friendly offices several times, and, being of the same language and religion, she naturally looks to them. Her people shudder at the thought of falling under a forced protectorate of any people of foreign language.

A nationality secured in the way suggested would open the way to practical and efficient co-operation in the administration of the local government, and of extending influence and control among the natives, would open the way for aid in the development of a system of finance, by which reliable and adequate revenue could be collected and administered. It would also open the way for the appoint-

ment, at the request of the Republic, of
explorers and specialists to explore the
territory and locate its wealth, and open
lines of communication, first, by ordinary
roads, then, by telegraph, and, later on, by
railways, — all in the interest of the
Republic, and of such friendly representatives of commerce as might desire to
develop trade. Another important matter would be advice and assistance in
proper emigration from the United States
and elsewhere. Whatever America cannot do herself, I believe England would
gladly co-operate in doing, at the suggestion of America, and Liberia is ready
and anxious to have such friendly aid
as these nations could properly and wisely
give.

With the exception of this little patch
of territory owned by the Republic of
Liberia, all the African continent, with
its 150,000,000 of black natives, is rapidly
passing under the rule of the white man.
This tremendous fact must be accepted as,
in the Providence of God, marking a new
era in the history of the black races.

They are to have their chance in their continental home for generations at least under the tutelage of white Governments.

Liberia, however, has existed for seventy-five years as a colony or nation. It is the Providential child of the best thought and prayers and help of thousands of Christian people whose convictions were clear and positive that in some organised way the millions of negroes in America should have a share in the redemption of Africa. I believe that conviction was of God, and I also believe that it is the duty of America and England to hear and heed the appeal of this child of Providence.

THE COMMERCE, RAILWAYS, AND TELEGRAPHS OF AFRICA.

THE COMMERCE, RAILWAYS, AND TELEGRAPHS OF AFRICA.

BY EDWARD HEAWOOD, M.A.,

Of the Royal Geographical Society.

THE great Desert of Sahara divides the African continent into two very distinct regions. To the north, we have a strip of country similar on the whole in climate and productions to the southern parts of Europe, with which, through the facilities of communications supplied by the Mediterranean, it has been brought into close relations almost since the dawn of history. To the south, on the contrary, the great bulk of the continent has for centuries been isolated by that great desert barrier, while, as regards by far the greatest part of its area, it differs *in toto* from North Africa, both in its climate, productions, and people. It is, therefore, to Africa south of the Sahara, and in particular to the tropical regions to

which the term "new world of the nineteenth century" above all applies, that
our attention will be directed in the present article.

In dealing with the commerce of Africa,
it is unavoidable that we should look to
the future rather than the present. The
total volume of trade of the whole continent, and especially of the area within the
tropics, is at present so insignificant, as
shown by the latest estimates, that the
question that perforce thrusts itself upon
our consideration is, whether the present
state of things is to continue, or whether
the future has in store that awakening to
participation in the life of the world which
may enable the African continent to take
a more equal place among the rest than it
does at present. It will, therefore, be
necessary to look briefly at some of the
causes which are responsible for the present backward condition of Africa.

Foremost among these is usually placed
the uniform outline of the continent, and
the absence of natural means of communication with the interior. But although

these certainly account for the isolation of the interior parts, they form an inadequate reason for the undeveloped condition of the coast-lands, — many of which possess great fertility, — except in so far as the unbroken nature of the coasts and the absence of outlying islands has not tended to the evolution of enterprising races of navigators, such as have sprung up in more favoured parts of the world. The reason is rather to be found (1) in the character of the inhabitants; (2) in the absence of valuable products which might attract merchants from other parts of the world.

Africa possesses few thrifty and industrious races, such as those of southern and eastern Asia, whose silks and muslins formed an article of trade with the West in very early times; nor, on the other hand, could its supplies of the precious metals, or its natural vegetable productions, vie with the riches of Mexico and Peru, or with the costly spices of the far East. Thus, while America and Asia offered an irresistible attraction to the merchants and adventurers of Europe, and poured untold wealth into their coffers, African commerce has remained in a state of complete stagnation down to our own day.

It by no means follows, however, that the outlook for the future must of necessity be equally gloomy. While the rich treasures of the East and West did their work in attracting European enterprise to those regions, they no longer form the sole or even the principal basis of commerce, vast as have been the strides made by it within the past century. If we examine a list of the exports of such countries as India or Brazil, we find that by far the larger part consists of plantation products, grown largely under European supervision, most of which Africa is equally capable of producing, when once a sufficient impetus is given by the enterprise of the white races. Of the leading articles exported by India during 1865–96, at least three-fifths (in value) consisted of such products as rice, raw cotton, oil-seeds, tea, coffee, and indigo, not including opium, or items such as hides, skins, and wool, for the production of which Africa is at least equally adapted. From Brazil, again, the great bulk of the exports consist of the five items, coffee, sugar, rubber, tobacco, and cotton, all of which are also supplied by tropical Africa. It is, no doubt, an advantage to these countries to have obtained so important a start in the race, while Africa has hitherto lagged behind.

We hear, too, of overproduction of some of these articles; but, with the ever-increasing wealth and population of the world, it may be supposed that the increasing demand will, in time, necessitate new fields of supply. That most of the products alluded to will thrive well in tropical Africa, has been abundantly shown by recent experiments in cultivation, notably by the successful introduction of coffee-growing into Nyassaland and elsewhere, while it has been proved that, although the tropical regions of the continent can never become the permanent home of the white man, many of the higher districts are sufficiently healthy to enable him to live in comparative comfort, and supply the energy and supervision which are absolutely necessary to any undertakings of the kind alluded to.

There is no doubt that agriculture is destined in future to be the mainstay of commercial prosperity for Africa, supposing that it is ever attained. The supply of ivory, which, together with slaves, has, in the past, formed the staple product of the continent, must, sooner or later, come to an end, while the best of the jungle products — palm-oil, orchilla-weed, wax, gums, etc. — are hardly like to meet with a much larger demand than at present. An exception must be made in the case of rubber, the trade in which has made rapid strides within the past few years; but with the careless methods of collection employed, it is becoming more and more evident that the natural supplies cannot hold out indefinitely, but that, for this too, systematic cultivation will become necessary before long.

In all attempts at cultivation the labour

question undoubtedly forms an important difficulty, owing to the unwillingness of the negro to work except for the supply of his own positive wants. It would carry us too far from the subject to enter fully into the question; suffice it to say, that the difficulty does not seem insurmountable. The introduction of Indian coolies will, in Africa as elsewhere, possibly prove the best solution, while it may be hoped that the example of their thrift and industry may in time induce the natives to throw off their habits of indolence. It would, of course, be preferable to make use of the negro races, if that were possible; and that this may be the case is shown by satisfactory reports from Nyassaland, where tribes like the Angoni (of Zulu affinities) have shown an unusual readiness to work, and have proved themselves both honest and industrious.

We have considered so far merely the question of the supply of products for export. We have now to examine briefly the prospects of a market being obtained in Central Africa for the productions of civilised nations. In this respect, also, Africa stands at a disadvantage by comparison with other continents, the wants of the natives, both in the way of clothing and any of the other adjuncts of civilised life, are at present so small that it will be long before any large demand for such articles will arise. It is among the races of the Central Sûdan, where Arab influence and civilisation have long made themselves felt, that we may expect that a market will be soonest obtained. The population is here unusually dense for Africa, while some of the races, notably the Hausas, are naturally keen traders. The Hausa caravans travel for long distances through the neighbouring countries, and have of late been pushing farther and farther south, having even penetrated as far as the French establishments in the Kongo Basin. Uganda is perhaps the next promising field for European trade, owing to its fairly dense population, and the remarkable readiness with which the inhabitants have imbibed European ideas.

Telegraphs of Africa.

One of the greatest obstacles to the development of African trade, at least with the interior regions, has of course been the entire absence of easy means of transport, that by native porters, which has until the last few years been almost the only method of conveying goods throughout the whole of tropical Africa, being far too costly to answer from a commercial point of view. This important defect is now being rapidly removed by the construction of railways, the progress made in which up to the present we shall shortly consider. First, however, it may be well to glance at the existing state of trade in the various European colonies and protectorates, and at the principal resources on which its future development, in each case, must depend.

Beginning with South Africa, which occupies a position of its own, first, from the fact that its climate permits of colonisation by the white men, and, secondly, from the great impetus given to trade by the recent development of mining industries, we find, for the Cape Colony and

238 Commerce, Railways,

Natal, according to the statistics for 1897 just published, a total volume of trade of somewhat over £47,000,000, divided almost equally between imports and exports, the latter being in excess in the Cape Colony, the former in Natal. This amount certainly far exceeds the total trade of the whole of tropical Africa, which was estimated by a well-informed writer in the London " Times," two years ago, to amount to little more than £17,000,000. It shows a great increase as compared with the total amount a few years back; in 1891, for instance, it reached a total of less than £25,000,000. The great bulk of the increase is, however, made up of exports of gold coming from the Transvaal, though other items, such as mohair, hides, and ostrich feathers, show a satisfactory gain. Wool, on the contrary, shows a considerable decline. A large proportion of the trade of the Transvaal and Orange Free State passes through the Cape Colony and Natal, and is thus included in the returns for those colonies. The rest passes through Lourenço Marquez, the Portuguese port of Delagoa Bay; but the exports by this route are very small, while of the imports, food-stuffs form a considerable item, showing the disregard to agriculture due to the gold fever. In the interests of the permanent prosperity of South Africa, it is to be hoped that, in future, trade may depend less than it does at present on the proceeds of the gold and diamond mines.

Turning now to tropical Africa, we find that it is only where jungle products are obtainable in large quantities, within easy distance of the coast, that the volume of trade has reached any considerable figure, and even here it is insignificant compared with that of flourishing colonies in other parts of the world. In the British West African colonies, — including the Niger Coast Protectorate, — where the exports have been swelled by large amounts of rubber, palm-oil, and palm-kernels, the total trade has not yet much exceeded £6,000,000. Lagos, the Gold Coast, and the Niger Coast Protectorate, each show a trade of between £1,500,000 and

£2,000,000, while that of Sierra Leone falls a little short of £1,000,000. Although these figures are very much higher than was the case a dozen years ago, the increase during the last three or four years has not been rapid, some articles of export, including palm-oil, even showing a falling off in certain of the colonies. The rubber industry has received a decided stimulus; but it is exceedingly doubtful whether the supply will not soon show signs of exhaustion. Satisfactory points are the rise in the total of imports, largely consisting of cottons, in spite of the reduced influx of spirits, and the increased export of such products as timber from the Gold Coast, and coffee, cocoa, arrowroot, etc., from the Gold Coast and Niger.

The trade of the interior Niger territories, peopled by the enterprising Hausa race, though possessing, perhaps, greater potentialities than any other part of Central Africa, has not yet assumed large proportions, being probably little over £1,000,000.

Of the French colonies, Senegal stands first with respect to volume of trade, which, however, probably does not exceed £1,500,000. In the vast region known as French Kongo, little advance has yet been made. Nor has any decided success attended the heroic efforts of the Belgians to develop the resources of the Kongo Free State, where the total imports and exports fall short of £1,000,000. Ivory and India-rubber form at present almost the sole products of the greater part of the area, but, with judicious management, the supply of both might last for a great number of years. It has been shown that both coffee and cocoa will thrive on the Upper Kongo; but many difficulties will have to be overcome before these can repay cultivation. Angola, though a very rich country, suffers from the want of encouragement to merchants on the part of the Portuguese Government. Its trade, though it has reached about £1,500,000, has of late not been in a satisfactory condition, having been injuriously affected by the fall in the price of coffee, which, with rubber and wax, forms the chief export. Of the German West African Colonies, the Kamerun has the most flourishing trade, amounting to nearly £500,000 in 1897. Spirits form a large item in the imports.

In East Africa, the principal trade-centre is, of course, Zanzibar, where, in 1896, the total trade with foreign countries amounted to nearly £2,500,000. This figure is, however, swelled by the fact that it includes a considerable transit trade with the mainland opposite, especially German East Africa. As regards its own proper trade, cloves form almost the only important article of export, and the island is at present suffering from overproduction, which has brought about a decline in the price of cloves. A satisfactory increase is reported in the import of piece goods. The trade of the mainland still remains within very narrow limits, though great possibilities exist. Thus, in British East Africa, the rubber trade only awaits encouragement to assume large proportions, while large supplies of copra, cotton, etc., could be produced. In British Central Africa, the outlook is encouraging, owing to the large measure of success attained in the cultivation of coffee, while in Uganda, although the trade is at present trifling, signs of increased activity were noticed before the outbreak of the recent disturbances. In German East Africa, in spite of the display of much energy in the establishment of plantations, the total trade has not yet exceeded £750,000. Coffee is the most paying product, but unfortunately the fungus known as *Hemeleia vastatrix* has found its way into the plantations. Farther south, the port of Beira, destined to serve as the outlet for Mashonaland, has lately sprung into being, and already shows signs of considerable activity.

It remains to speak of the progress which has been made of late years in opening up communication with the interior of Africa by means of railways and telegraphs, which have now been recognised as indispensable aids to the extension of commercial intercourse throughout the continent. Owing to the manner in which its surface has been parcelled out among the European nations, it has come about that almost each colony or protectorate has its own scheme for a railway, destined to bring down the produce of its hinterland for shipment at its principal port. For Central Africa, the earliest schemes were those intended to re-enforce the navigable portions of streams as means of communication. Thus, in Senegal, the French, some years ago, constructed a line from the port of Dakar to the Lower Senegal, and commenced the construction of another from Kayes, at the head of the navigation on that river, across to the Upper Niger. Great difficulties were encountered in this second section, and progress ceased for a time, when the line had reached Bafulabe, at the junction of the two main branches of the Senegal. In 1895 work was resumed, and the line has now crossed the Bafing, and reached a place called Diubeba, about thirty miles beyond. Its gauge is one metre. Lately a new project has been started, which, if carried out, will somewhat detract from the importance of the existing line; it has been proposed to build a railway through from Konakry, on the coast of the Upper Niger, a distance no greater than that to be traversed by the line from Kayes.

The great difficulty encountered by most of the African railway schemes is the fact that they all have to negotiate the crossing of the difficult outer escarpments of the interior plateau. Thus the Kongo Railway, intended to supply means of communication past the rapids of the lower river, has involved an enormous outlay and has proceeded exceedingly slowly. The greatest difficulties have been, however, at last surmounted, and the line has now come within measurable distance of its goal, — Stanley Pool. According to the report of Major Thys, in December last, it had reached the 348th kilometre, out of a total of 388. A considerable traffic already exists on the portion completed, and there can be no doubt that when once trains reach the Upper Kongo, with its thousands of miles of navigable waterways, a great impetus will be given to trade. While on the subject of the Kongo, it may be mentioned that new schemes have lately been set on foot for railway construction in the remoter parts of the basin, — in the northeast, southeast, and in the region of the Rapids of the Mobangi, the great northern tributary.

Another railway which has been under construction for some years is that starting from St. Paul de Loanda, the capital of Angola, toward Ambaka and Malange. Difficulties in the way of bridging the· streams have here too caused delays; but it is hoped the line will in August next be completed to the end of its first section, the Lukalla River. The receipts per kilometre on the mileage open have steadily risen during the last few years. The company constructing this line bears the ambitious title of " Royal Company of Trans-African Railways," it being hoped that a junction may be ultimately effected by its means with the Portuguese East Africa Colonies. More recent West African schemes are those for lines starting inland from Sierra Leone, Lagos, and Swakopmund, the new port of German Southwest Africa. Some progress has been made with each of these, while railway surveys have also been carried out on the Gold Coast.

Passing now to East Africa, we come to the important schemes for linking the coast with the great interior lakes. Both Germans and British have for some years aimed at connecting their coast settlements with the Victoria Nyanza; and it seemed at one time as if the former would carry through their project while the latter were deliberating. At last, however, the British scheme has been taken up energetically by the Government, and the progress so far has been rapid. Starting from Mombasa, the line has already passed the 120th mile, and has proved of value in facilitating the passage of the Taru Desert; but the country lying ahead, especially at the Kikuya encampment, will present more difficulties than those hitherto encountered. The route has, however, been carefully surveyed, and, with the efficient base of operations provided, it may be hoped that progress will continue to be rapid, and that in another five or six years the line will have reached its terminus at Port Alice in Berkeley Bay, Lake Victoria, 656 miles from Mombasa. Not till this occurs can any great development in the trade of Uganda be looked for. In German East Africa, a short line of railway already penetrates inland, toward the borders of Usambara, but funds have not yet been provided for a more extended scheme. The idea most favoured is the construction of a line from Dar-es-Salaam to Ujiji, on Lake Tanganyika, with a branch northward from Tabora to Lake Victoria. An important scheme has been set on foot in British Central Africa, — Nyassaland, — for the making of a short railway across the Shiré Highlands so as to supply communication past the rapids by which the Shiré River is obstructed. This would materially improve what is known as the "Lakes Route" into Central Africa. Toward the north, the French have commenced the construction of a line from their port of Dijibouti, on the Red Sea, to the important town of Harrar, subject to the King of Abyssinia; while the Italians have opened a short line inland from Massaua. From Suakim also a line is certain to be made by the British either to Berber or to Kassala.

In South Africa, an important system of railways, starting from the ports of Cape Colony, Natal, and Delagoa Bay, and making for the mining districts of Kimberley and the Transvaal, is already in full working order, though new lines are being now added. More nearly bearing on our subject are the new lines destined to serve as highways to the rising settlements in Mashonaland and Matabeleland. The one of these which forms the continuation of the Cape line to Kimberley and Mafeking was opened through to Buluwayo on November 4th, 1897, having been completed in a wonderfully short space of time considering its length; the other, which starts from Beira on the East Coast, and is to end at Salisbury, in Mashonaland, has not made such rapid progress, but has passed Chimoio, near the frontier, between British and Portuguese territory. A proposal has been made to unite Salisbury and Buluwayo by railway, and thus complete the circuit between the East and South Coasts.

A brief mention only can be made of the telegraph lines which have accompanied, and in some instances preceded, the lines of railway lately opened or planned. Both in East and West Africa, for instance, the Portuguese possessions have been provided with short lines, while, in British East Africa, one running northward from Mombasa to Lamu has been opened for several years; but the most important line of all, and the one which has progressed most rapidly, is that which owes its inception to the energy of Mr. Cecil Rhodes, and goes by the name of the African Transcontinental Telegraph Line. Starting from the Cape, it makes its way to Buluwayo and Salisbury, and thence *via* Umtali to Tete on the Zambezi. It then cuts across to the Shiré River, and has already ascended the west shore of Lake Nyassa as far as Kota Kota. By the end of 1898 it is thought that it will reach the south end of Lake Tanganyika, while an extension still farther northward is proposed, so that it may eventually reach the Nile and form an uninterrupted chain between the two extremities of the continent. It is said that the newly opened section in Nyassaland is already used by the natives for communication with friends at a distance.

THE MAP OF AFRICA.

THE MAP OF AFRICA.

BY H. K. CARROLL, LL.D.

THE map of Africa has undergone wonderful, indeed, revolutionary, changes in the last half century. Except in outline and certain general features, the Africa of 1898 bears little resemblance to the Africa of 1848. The changes are due, first, to the results of exploration, secondly, to the European greed for territory.

It is rather strange that so large a portion of the continent should have remained unknown to the rest of the world until the last half of the present century. Africa was known for ages and ages before the Western world was discovered. We speak of America as new, but Africa is as old as civilisation or human history. When the United States celebrated, in 1876, the first centenary of its independence, this message was received from Egypt (I quote from memory):

"The oldest country of the world sends greetings to the youngest."

Egyptian civilisation was second to none in antiquity, unless, possibly, to that of Babylonia. The Nile, its great physical feature, has been the geographical puzzle of the centuries, from, if not before, Ptolemy to Stanley, to whom the honour of its solution belongs. The great explorer found its source not far from where the old Egyptian geographer conjectured it to be. Ptolemy's idea was that the mighty artery came from the heart of the continent, rising in two lakes lying 4° or 5 south of the equator. The fact is, it rises in the Victoria Nyanza, nearly all of which is below the equator, though it does not reach the fourth degree. The second lake is, of course, the Albert, which, however, is not a source, as Sir Samuel Baker supposed, but only a back-water of the Nile. It will be noticed that the smaller map, representing Africa as it appeared in atlases fifty years ago, has no indication of these lakes, nor of those of Tanganyika and Nyassa farther to the south.

These are a part of the results of recent exploration.

One of the notable features of all the older maps is a chain of mountains represented as extending across the continent from east to west, about five degrees north of the equator. In these fabled mountains, perhaps suggested by Mts. Kenia and Kilimanjaro, the Nile was supposed, as will be seen by the accompanying map, to have its rise. The mythical mountains disappear, and the Kongo is shown to be a much mightier river than the old map-makers knew. It does for South and Equatorial Africa what the Nile does for the northeastern quarter of the continent, drains an immense territory. Above the cataracts, by the side of which a railroad has been constructed, the noble river, with its many long tributaries, aggregating thousands of miles of navigable stream offers to commerce abundant transportation facilities, and opens a country unknown to Europeans until the intrepid Stanley explored it.

One now looks in vain for the equatorial

country known for centuries to African map-makers as "Ethiopia." The great native kingdom of Uganda occupies part of the territory that bore the ancient and honourable name, and the rest of it is gathered into the State of Kongo, and "Ethiopia," with the "Mountains of the Moon" as its northern boundary, disappears forever, probably. Thus do the practical geographers of the closing century sweep away ruthlessly some of the most characteristic features of the old African maps.

The new Africa has no "unexplored regions" inhabited by all manner of ferocious four-footed beasts and creeping things. Elephants and lions and gorillas and reptiles there are in abundance; but the spaces in old maps which were adorned with pictures of them are now filled with details of rivers, lakes, mountains, towns, and tribes. Fifty years ago, not even the location of tribes was known. "Wandering Bushmen" were indicated as having penetrated as far north as the equator, 2,000 miles or more beyond the territory where they are actually found. Living-

stone, Stanley, and other active explorers
have left but little for their successors to
discover. Africa is no longer a *terra incognita*, and, while minor details remain to
be settled by more leisurely and better
equipped expeditions, nothing of great
importance is likely to be revealed as to
the geographical features of the continent.

The political changes have been quite
as remarkable as those due to exploration,
and much more extensive. Unappropri-
ated Africa is now only a comparatively
inconsiderable portion of the whole continent. There are two sections, one lying
between Egypt and the French Sahara and
Tripoli and the tenth degree of north latitude, and the other on the right bank
of the Upper Niger, which as yet wear
no European colour. They appear on the
map as light yellow. The Niger territory
will, however, soon be divided between
France and England, if the Anglo-French
Commission, sitting in Paris, can reach an
agreement. Doubtless the larger part will
a few months hence be annexed to the
immense French territory which surrounds

it on the north and west. England would be satisfied if she could have the triangular strip indicated by the dotted lines running south from Say to the border-line between English Lagos and French Dahomey, and with a reasonable hinterland for its Gold Coast Territory. Within a year the lines between French Dahomey and German Togoland have been changed, so that the latter now extends north to and including Gambaga, and west to the White Volta River. This extension is somewhat faintly indicated on the map.

Doubtless the British red, which covers Egypt and Nubia, will be extended erelong to the northern border of British East Africa, thus making the Nile a British stream from source to delta. The French Marchand expedition, whose purpose was to annex some of the Nile territory, appears to have met with defeat. At last accounts, nearly all the force had deserted the indomitable Frenchman, who still refused to abandon entirely his enterprise.

Abyssinia appears in our map with

much larger territory than it was represented as having in most other maps, published as late even as January 1st, 1898.
It was then represented as lying within
the Italian Sphere of Influence, with British East Africa for the western and southern boundary, and the Indian Ocean for
the eastern. Abyssinia has emerged an
independent kingdom with greatly enlarged boundaries, and the Italian possessions have shrunken to the province of
Eritrea, on the Red Sea, and Somaliland,
on the Indian Ocean. The portion
printed in deep colour indicates Abyssinia
proper; the rest is territory conceded to
Menelek by English and Italian treaties.
Adis Adaba has just been made the
capital.

There are six countries bearing the tint
of Abyssinia, — Morocco, Liberia, Kongo,
South African Republic, and Orange Free
State, besides Menelek's kingdom. These
are classed as independent native States,
although Kongo is really as much Belgian
as Egypt is English. These are the only
native States remaining. All the rest, ex-

cept the yellow tinted desert west of Egypt, is under European control. In the last half century nearly the whole continent has been divided up between England, France, Belgium, and Germany; and even the two Republics in South Africa are dominated by a population of European origin, and the Transvaal owes suzerainty to England.

Fifty years ago England had only the extreme southern end of the continent, with small holdings on the West Coast north of the equator. Now its possessions are well-nigh continuous from Cape Town to Alexandria; and it is the dream of Cecil Rhodes to connect the two at no distant day by telegraph, and to consolidate, in one magnificent empire of British South Africa, all the territory south of Lake Nyassa, save the German and Portuguese possessions.

France had only Senegal and Algiers at the date when the smaller map was made. Portugal had the same coast-line then as now; she has only added hinterlands to her Angola and Mozambique territories.

Turkey still holds Tripoli, but has lost
Tunis and, practically, Egypt.   Spain has
made no appreciable gain.   Germany,
Italy, and Belgium are altogether newcomers.

In the eighteenth century the civilised
world was engaged, some one has said, in
stealing Africans from Africa, while in the
nineteenth it has been stealing Africa
from the Africans.   How thoroughly this
has been accomplished is shown by the
accompanying map.

www.ingramcontent.com/pod-product-compliance
Lightning Source LLC
Chambersburg PA
CBHW030340270326
41926CB00009B/902